I believe there is MORE!
Tom S Morgan

MORE!
Moving Into an Arena of Spiritual Power

MORE!

Moving Into an Arena of Spiritual Power

TOBY S. MORGAN

PATHWAY PRESS

Scripture quotations, unless otherwise indicated, are taken from the *New King James Version*. Copyright © 1979, 1980, 1982, 1990, 1995 by Thomas Nelson, Inc., Publishers.

Scripture quotations marked NIV are taken from the *Holy Bible, New International Version*®. *NIV*®. Copyright © 1973, 1978, 1984 by International Bible Society. Used by permission of Zondervan Publishing House. All rights reserved.

Scripture quotations marked TM are taken from *The Message*. Copyright © by Eugene H. Peterson 1993, 1994, 1995, 1996, 2000, 2001, 2002. Used by permission of NavPress Publishing Group.

Scripture quotations marked KJV are taken from the King James Version of the Bible.

Editorial staff: Lance Colkmire, Tom George, Tammy Hatfield, and Esther Metaxas

Edited by Tom George

Cover design and graphics by Michael McDonald

Inside pages design by Tom George

ISBN: 9781596847163

Copyright © 2012 by Pathway Press
1080 Montgomery Avenue
Cleveland, TN 37311

All rights reserved. No part of this publication may be reproduced or transmitted in any form or by any means, electronic or mechanical, including photocopying, recording, or otherwise, or by any information storage or retrieval system, without the permission in writing from the publisher. Please direct inquiries to Pathway Press, 1080 Montgomery Avenue, Cleveland, TN 37311.

Visit *www.pathwaypress.org* for more information.

Printed in the United States of America

CONTENTS

Introduction		7
Chapter 1	MORE!	13
Chapter 2	There Is MORE Available	25
Chapter 3	Intoxicating Power	35
Chapter 4	What Can I Expect?	51
Chapter 5	Restoration	59
Chapter 6	When Things Are Really Bad!	71
Chapter 7	How to Get Back	87
Chapter 8	Keep Coming!	107
Chapter 9	A Message to the Leaders	119

INTRODUCTION

In the year 586 BC, Nebuchadnezzar destroyed Jerusalem, the capital city of Israel. Jeremiah had wept like a baby over what he saw coming: "How lonely sits the city that was full of people! How like a widow is she, who was great among the nations! The princess among the provinces has become a slave! . . . Her adversaries have become the master, her enemies prosper; for the Lord has afflicted her because of the multitude of her transgressions. Her children have gone into captivity before the enemy" (Lam. 1:1, 5).

In spite of their status as chosen people, the decided advantage of having the very presence of Jehovah in their midst, they watched it all ebb away and suddenly it all crashed down on them. Even their vaunted religious institutions, rife with ritual and ceremony, meant nothing. They walked away from God and stepped directly into exile.

Fast-forward seventy years. The names of men like Ezra and Nehemiah began to cross the darkened horizon. It seemed God was up to something once more in the Holy City. Buildings began to be reclaimed, and walls began to see repair. Men and women were beginning to sense a hunger for the Word of God. The sweet aroma of revival was once more in the air as they were witnessing a resurgence of passion for God. Most likely, a young man descended from a priestly family by the name of Zechariah was just beginning to take notice of these events.

Fast-forward again, this time about sixteen years. The foundations of the Temple had been laid. What once appeared to be a great revival, a "new day," had stalled out. Somewhere along the way, something had happened. What most thought should have been so easy had become difficult indeed.

For sixteen years, they had struggled with unrealized expectations. Things just hadn't turned out the way they thought they should. It amazes me how true to life their story is. Haven't we all sensed we were on the verge of something great from God, heard the hopeful prophecies that "blessing was on the way," only to hit a brick wall of unrealized expectations? Consider for a moment what this group of saints had to deal with.

First, they had to combat the discouraging notion that everyone wasn't on board with their new revival. Yes, God had opened up a clear pathway for His people to leave the land of bondage and come home. They were given a chance to walk once more in the paths of the greats of yesterday. But the simple fact was ... some of them decided they were so comfortable in the environs of captivity they had no desire to risk the rigors of moving into a new walk with God. Regrettably, this mentality hasn't changed through the centuries. Scarcely exists a pastor who, upon having a new wave of glory come upon his church, has not had to endure the agonizing pain of separation as members of his church, often some of his closest friends, decide to move on to another locale rather than make the adjustments necessary to flow in the Spirit.

Second, they had to confront trouble at home. Being disappointed from afar wasn't enough; they quickly discovered not everyone living next door was thrilled about this new push for revival. This too hasn't changed. Find a place, a location where revival has come, and you will find people within the church who are less than happy with the newfound joy others are encountering. Again, find a pastor who has witnessed an outbreak of God's glory who, in turn, hasn't had to face the lions of discouragement from some of his own church members, and you will be looking at a rare individual indeed!

The result in Zechariah's day was much the same we see today. While God had every intention of doing mighty things in their midst, they became disheartened and the work of the Lord stalled. It didn't completely disappear; it just ground to a halt. They still had church—Temple worship—but the passion for the greater things of God was gone. In other words, they just stalled out and settled for average.

Here's what the Lord had to say to them about two months before Zechariah pops onto the stage: "Go up to the mountains and bring wood and build the temple, that I may take pleasure in it and be glorified," says the Lord. "You looked for much, but indeed it came to little; and when you brought it home, I blew it away. Why?" says the Lord of hosts. "Because of My house that is in ruins, while every one of you runs to his own house" (Hag. 1:8-9).

They hadn't completely abandoned God; they had just moved Him down a notch or two in order of importance. They hadn't stopped noticing God; they had simply made Him a lesser priority. The result was, they had lost the blessing of the Lord. Amazing . . . they were living in a time of great outpouring, of intense activity from heaven, but they had settled into a rut of mediocrity!

We can deny it, decry it, or denounce those who point it out, but we in the American church sit in the same seat as did the recipients of Zechariah's visionary words. In spite of all our "megachurches," packed conferences, and celebrity pastors—all the stuff we point to when someone tries to talk honestly with us about our lack of power and passion—a close examination of us, the American church, reveals we are frighteningly lacking. No need to bore you with statistics, although some are sprinkled through this work.

It doesn't take one long, while traveling through our nation, to see an illuminating fact: *the American church is dying!* If you don't believe me, take a few Sundays, leave your cozy nest where you go to church, drive around during church hours, and actually open your eyes to this fact: the vast majority of people in America are not even close to going to a church. We live today in what missionologists call the "third-largest mission field" on the planet. We have accomplished that lofty perch with churches everywhere, more visibility for the gospel than any nation has ever witnessed, and a plethora of ministers so well known they rival national political leaders in recognition. And perhaps most condemning of all, having gone through an attack on our national shores several years back that seemed to drive people to us, only to have us standing, wringing our hands, as they walked away as suddenly as they appeared once the national conscience was soothed.

It doesn't take a prophet to see this glaring truth. Something isn't working. We have stalled out . . . sputtered to a stop. Like those living in Jerusalem after the initial surge of Ezra and Nehemiah had faded to the background, we have allowed the disappointments and disillusionments of our day to cause us to settle for just what we have. But that wasn't God's plan for them, nor is it His design for us!

Onto the stage stepped a young man, Zechariah. He came, not in his own priestly lineage, though he had those credentials. Neither did he come in his own ingenuity or slick presentations. He came with precisely what we so desperately need today—the word of the Lord! "Therefore say to them, 'Thus says the Lord of hosts: "Return to Me," says the Lord of hosts, "and I will return to you," says the Lord of hosts'" (Zech. 1:3).

In essence, that's his entire message. Zechariah told them about visions, which are amazing. Let's be honest—if someone showed up at virtually any church in America today and claimed such interaction with heaven, if he weren't immediately ushered to the street, he would claim the attention of the burliest usher!

In most cases, he would be treated like the man I read about years ago. It seemed he showed up, unknown to all, dressed in a Superman suit, cape and all! He walked in, with everyone naturally staring, marched down the aisle, and sat squarely on the front pew in plain sight of the bewildered pastor. Of course the pastor, caught off guard, didn't know what to do. In a moment, a kindly old gentleman, one of the ushers, walked down, sat by the superhero want-to-be, and whispered something into his ear. In a flash, "Superman" was up, down the aisle, and without a fuss, out the door. Later, the pastor had to know how the stately gentleman had handled the explosive situation. "I told him to be careful . . . our pews are lined with Kryptonite," said the sly elder.

That solution would probably be the desired effect in most of our churches if Zechariah showed up—a quiet resolution that ruffles no feathers . . . a hasty dispatch that ensures smooth sailing for all involved. And while that solution is great for those who are a little off-center, I fear we have decided anyone with a message that causes us discomfort, who challenges us to a renewed passion for God—dare I say, anyone who claims God still has the ability to amaze us—is greeted with virtually the same skepticism and scorn as a man showing up in a Superman costume.

Sadly, the man probably wouldn't be welcome in most churches. Zechariah's visions, eight of them, are sometimes convoluted and difficult to grasp. Yet when viewed from a distance, they all come together to reveal a message which is so needed today. In essence, Zechariah told his fellow travelers: "No matter how bad it appears at the moment, no matter how far away from God's plan His people might be at this moment, God will do what needs to be done to see His glory manifested and His purpose brought to pass."

That is the message we—the stumbling, weary, settling-for-"whatever" American church—need to hear. We might not like it, might not even want to hear it, but it's the only thing that offers us hope. Mark this down, etch it in stone, and remember you read it here: *The only thing offering the American church any hope whatsoever is a wholehearted return to Him and His subsequent rush to us!*

Go to all the conferences, buy all the books and tapes, and stand in long lines to get into the "mega" events. Enjoy yourself—there is nothing wrong with any of that. But know this: *If we don't quit playing our games and get serious about getting back to Him, the generation alive today will witness the decline of the church in America just like our brothers and sisters in the faith have seen through the centuries in their native lands!*

THE RAINBOW IN THE RAIN

The good news is, it doesn't have to be that way. We can change the very destiny of our land, our lives, and our church. God spoke something through Zechariah that offers so much hope, so much promise, it's thrilling to just step back and take it all in. It isn't found in a vision the young prophet received. Rather, it's a challenge uttered from the Throne to a bewildered people: "Ask the Lord for rain in the time of the latter rain. The Lord will make flashing clouds; He will give them showers of rain, grass in the field for everyone" (Zech. 10:1).

I need a shower. Actually, I need more than a shower. I need a deluge from on high that sweeps me up and carries me away. I need so much of His outpouring that I can't contain it. How about you?

It's His promise—to them, and to us. And, as we are going to see, it's one He will keep. MORE, Lord!

Chapter 1

MORE!

Ask the Lord for rain in the time of the latter rain. The Lord will make flashing clouds; He will give them showers of rain, grass in the field for everyone. For the idols speak delusion; the diviners envision lies, and tell false dreams; they comfort in vain. Therefore the people wend their way like sheep; they are in trouble because there is no shepherd. "My anger is kindled against the shepherds, and I will punish the goatherds. For the Lord of hosts will visit His flock, the house of Judah, and will make them as His royal horse in the battle" (Zech. 10:1-3).

If ever a nation, or a church, needed to receive and act on this staggering call from God, the nation or church of which we in America are a part certainly fit the bill. There are so many striking similarities to the situation facing Zechariah, and the condition in which we find ourselves today, that one cannot help but be excited at the promise of God to bring into our lives far more than we currently experience. Like the church in Zechariah's day, we have done some very good things and made some really great strides. We have dotted the landscape of America with posh palaces of worship, just as they eventually erected a Temple when they came back from captivity. Ezra had raised the bar when it came to godly living, and we have teachers imploring us to heed the commands and promises of God. One would think that all these blessings—all the great things we have seen from the hand of God—would propel us to further greatness. Sadly, such doesn't seem to be the case.

Something seems to be missing. By and large, the church in America goes through the motions, content if enough "noses and nickels" are present each week to keep the machinery running. We have a cottage industry of "church-growth experts," all telling us the latest means and methods of reaching an ever-greater harvest, each pointing to the sterling success stories of their particular method.

Even with all the above advantages, the church is falling further and further behind. Our impact on our culture has been lost, and we are swiftly being relegated to the fringe margins of society. We are tolerated at best, loathed at worst.

Most Christians from the overwhelming majority of churches are *passionless* about their walk with God. Recently, I was in a Jehovah's Witness church for a business transaction. Yet, while I was there, they made an effort to convert me. The man was passionate about his church... his beliefs. Sadly, you won't find that type of passion very much these days from most church members. A lack of passion makes us useless to God. Search the Scriptures... you'll never find anyone making a difference for God who didn't possess passion.

We have become *powerless* as well. Confronted by an ever-increasing pall of spiritual darkness, today's church chooses to meet supernatural foes with natural weapons. We are discovering what we have really known all along. To deal with the devil and his weapons, we must be possessors of God's powerful tools.

As much as we hate to admit it, the church has become *profitless* to the Kingdom. Sure, we are experts at staging great events, but what about setting the captive free? Make no mistake, we have excelled at illumining a few of the ills of society, usually our "hobbyhorse" sins, but where are the priests and prophets who weep inconsolably for our sons and daughters who have fallen prey to the very sins we so blatantly denounce? If we are going to be honest—and I am convinced no revival comes until we are brutally honest—we have to admit we have lost something in the American church. We have lost something in my church.

But the Prophet Says . . .

Some may be thinking even now: *Just another curmudgeon who is mad because time is passing him by!* I wish that were so. But, as the late Ronald Reagan used to say, "Facts are stubborn things." And the facts are, in spite of all the blessing and prosperity prophets, in spite of all the church-growth gurus, something's just not right in the church.

Consider some telling facts which are so obvious, it's a wonder we aren't doing something:

- In the past thirty years or so, the population of our country has grown by some fifty million people.
- In today's America, about 65 percent of our population is unchurched, with no formal connection whatsoever.
- We have the largest generation in the history of the world to grow up outside the influence of the church.
- No county in America has seen a 1 percent increase in church attendance over the last ten years. As a matter of fact, of the 3,098 counties in America, 2,303 have actually declined in church attendance!
- Right now, the United States ranks third in the world for need of missionaries. Just think of it, for decades we sent missionaries around the globe. Now, God is bringing the mission harvest to our backdoor—and we are shrinking from the task.
- While many like to point to the growing churches—the mega churches—the fact is only 15 percent of the churches in our country are growing. Before you get excited, hear this: 14 percent are growing due to transfer growth; only 1 percent grows due to people coming to Christ.

- Statisticians tell us if current trends continue, 60 percent of existing churches in America will be gone by the year 2050.

To argue that we are strong, that we are getting along just fine, and that we don't need a fresh visit from heaven is so delusional and frightening to consider. Still, there are those who maintain with devoted vigilance that there is nothing wrong with our churches that a few adjustments in programs and presentation won't fix. We don't need to have anything that smacks of the supernatural—we are doing just fine without such action. That sounds very much like the day of Zechariah, when there were those who were continually telling the people, "All is well!" Of course, this was nothing new. The Old Testament lays out a pattern of behavior among Israel. They would listen to false teachers, men who always had a "good word," a "blessing word." Coupled with this empty rhetoric, they would usually cast aside any man of God with a challenging word of repentance. The result was predictable: they would drift—lose their passion, power, and profit—and wind up in desperate times. Over and over again, they (to borrow Paul's warning about our day) "heaped up teachers who told them only what they wanted to hear" (see 2 Tim. 4:3). Of course, in the crucible of life, away from the showy presentations of these false teachers, the doctrines they put forth fell short.

Zechariah was harsh with such tactics. He used strong words: *delusion, lies, falsehoods*. One allusion he used was to compare their teachings to vapor. He considered their words as nothing but hot air! Make no mistake, false teaching about God, giving us a sense of ease when we should be in repentance, may very well make us feel better about ourselves and may even give us a false high for the moment; but it *always* leads to some form of self-deception and eventual captivity.

MORE!

It was into precisely such a situation, strikingly similar to ours, that God thundered from heaven and commanded His people to do something totally out of character . . . out of place. *In the middle of the rainy season, while it was pouring out rain, God called upon them to ask Him for MORE!* Think of it, while it was in the season of the latter rains, God nudged them and compelled them to ask Him for more rain.

Sounds almost selfish, doesn't it? Here you are in the middle of something great, the "latter rain," and you want more. One evening I went to one of those "pay-the-price-and-eat-all-you-can" restaurants. I was alone, so I became engrossed in watching people. I watched dozens of people who really didn't need to be in such an establishment in the first place, going back to the food bar time and time again. Some went back so much, each time carrying one (sometimes two) plates which needed sideboards; it was a veritable festival of eating too much! Yet, that's what God is telling you and me to do. Here we are in the middle of arguably the greatest revival in the history of mankind around the world, and God is telling us to ask Him for MORE.

We need more. God wouldn't tell us to ask for it if we didn't need it. Today's church has become characterized by *arrogance*. We proudly point to a few success stories, some palatial buildings, the staggering amount of money some organizations take in, and never stop a moment to think we have just used the very measuring sticks that the world we are supposed to withdraw from uses to judge success! We blatantly display our *ignorance* of God's purpose and calling when we salute the successes of the past, all the while stepping over seas of lost people, never even being moved enough to pray for them. We demonstrate our *insolence* toward God when we brazenly live as if we don't care what He has to say about things. It's our church, and we will run it the way we see fit!

I haven't been able to shake the images of two churches from that famous list in the Revelation. Either of these two would be darlings of today's church culture. They were great churches, no doubt. Yet Jesus took the time to correct both!

First, consider Ephesus with its powerful history. Many things were still taking place. The church had been pastored by great men such as James, a brother of Jesus. Really, you can't get much better than that! But there was a problem in this great church: "Nevertheless I have this against you, that you have left your first love" (Rev. 2:4).

Now, I must confess I have misquoted that verse more times than I want to remember. I have twisted it and inserted the word *lost* in the place of the word *left*. There is a great deal of difference. The word used here means something deliberate. This wasn't some accidental, indiscriminate event. It was a choice—or better yet, a series of choices—which was made, resulting in abandonment. It was more like a divorce than misplacing the keys.

Then, there was the church at Laodicea. Jesus didn't have much good to say about this bunch. We are probably all familiar with His derision hurled at them: "So then, because you are lukewarm, and neither cold nor hot, I will vomit you out of My mouth" (3:16).

Not a very pleasant thought—making Jesus so sick at His stomach He wants to throw up! It goes without saying, the Lord wasn't too happy with them.

Yet, right here, in spite of all the junk they had going on, despite the fact they were useless—*Jesus tells them what to do!* "Behold, I stand at the door and knock. If anyone hears My voice and opens the door, I will come in to him and dine with him, and he with Me" (v. 20). If they will simply open the door and let Him in, and that means accepting Him in all His glory, they will no longer be the tepid, useless crowd that makes Him sick; they will become dinner partners with the King!

That screams to me, "There's hope!" All is not lost . . . we, I, can turn back to God our whole heart, and He will graciously receive and restore. While He is pouring out His Spirit in unprecedented fashion around the globe, we in America can call out for MORE and He will produce thunder and lightning in our lives.

Our Hope

I am convinced a fresh move of God is our only hope. Our way of rescue has always been right before us. God said, "If My people who are called by My name will humble themselves, and pray and seek My face, and turn from their wicked ways, then I will hear from heaven, and will forgive their sin and heal their land" (2 Chron. 7:14).

The solution for what ails the church is not a better army, flashier programs, higher scores in schools, or a more educated clergy. There is nothing wrong with those, per se, but they won't address the deep need of the church. Our hope will not be found in the political arena. The cozy marriage of the church with politicos has taught us one thing: No matter what they say, when it comes to the name of Jesus, they will court our vote and then act like His name is anathema. Our hope isn't found in the financial institutions of the world. For years we have been cozy with Wall Street and turned our heads to the greed and sleazy actions of those who lived in ways the Bible condemned, all so we could share in the salad days of money. God grabbed our attention, didn't He? The *Atlanta Journal Constitution* recently disclosed nearly one hundred churches in metro Atlanta that are facing foreclosure, while the *Wall Street Journal* presented an even direr picture, citing dozens of church foreclosures recently, whereas there had only been a small trickle of such actions in the past decades.

No, our hope has never been found in the institutions of man. Our hope rests solidly in the Lord, the One who calls to us amid our wandering and says, "There's more for you; if you will call to Me, you can have it." May He find us desperate in His presence for MORE of His glory.

There is more. Surely no one is possessed of such hauteur as to believe they have everything possible from God. Come on, no one is perfect, right? That admission being made, here are a few areas where we might discover God actually has more for us than we currently possess.

What about *rejoicing*? One of the major factors leading to powerlessness in today's church is the loss of the passion to rejoice. Hear again the words of the psalmist: "Will You not revive us again, that Your people may rejoice in You?" (Ps. 85:6).

Stop and think about what the majority of rejoicing in today's church centers on. People rejoice about their job. I have watched people go ballistic in church as they testified about receiving an unexpected financial boon. Who hasn't witnessed an eruption of emotion when someone's body is touched and they no longer feel pain? Haven't you been part of a crowd which grew ecstatic when a testimony was given about how God extracted someone from a rather sticky situation? That's the American church. That's what we are addicted to, and that's what sells in American religion. The result? We have lost our ability to rejoice in God—not God's stuff, but God.

The Hebrew phrase "in you" means "to be transfixed." No movement, no distraction, no motion. Basically, it is telling us revival will cause us to become fixated on God.

For too long we have become fixated on the religious trappings in which we have ensconced God. We have become addicted to His "stuff," and lost the ability to rejoice in nothing but Him. That is why we have churches filled with grumpy souls who refuse to rejoice because they are mad that things haven't gone their way. Perhaps the temperature in the church isn't set to their liking. Maybe the music doesn't fit their taste. Perhaps they didn't get their way in some business meeting. Thus, their view of God has become distorted; He is no longer worthy of praise because He, in their mind, has let them down.

Sure, we might lighten up and rejoice a little if someone levitates, spins around, or does something that triggers a deep emotion within us. But, how long has it been since you rejoiced in the simple fact God chose you? How long since you reveled in the simple act of God's plan to send His Son to die for you, His glory in awakening you to your need of His salvation, and the wondrous act of His forgiveness in your life!

Say what you will about the generations preceding us. However, they possessed something we do not . . . they would meet in ramshackle buildings most churches wouldn't consider using for a moment. Study Azusa Street and find out for yourself what that building was. Here's a hint . . . at one time it housed horses. They would sit on hard benches in freezing rooms heated by the old potbellied stove, or sweat like crazy in oven-like buildings with no air-conditioning, all the while waving those funeral-home fans like windmills. They had nothing of this world and wanted none of it. With no political connections, no money in the bank, and no real hopes of possessing either, they endured the elements as well as the sneers and jeers of the religious establishment. But they knew how to come together and rejoice in God! The joy of the Lord was their strength. It was the joy of the Lord—their ability to rejoice in the face of harshness—that brought them through the difficult valleys.

Remember, this is our heritage . . . not just Pentecostals or Charismatics, but all who claim the Bible as their foundation. One of my favorite passages reveals just what happens when a group of believers, possessing nothing but the ability to rejoice in God, is confronted by powers beyond their ability to withstand:

> And being let go, they went to their own companions and reported all that the chief priests and elders had said to them. So when they heard that, they raised their voice to God with one accord and said: Lord, You are God, who made heaven and earth and the sea, and all that is in them, who by the mouth of Your servant David have said: 'Why did the nations rage, and the people plot vain things? The kings of the earth took their stand, and the rulers were gathered together against the Lord and against His Christ.' For truly against Your holy Servant Jesus, whom You anointed, both Herod and Pontius Pilate, with the Gentiles and the people of Israel, were gathered together to do whatever Your hand and Your purpose determined before to be done. Now, Lord, look on their threats, and grant to Your servants that with all boldness they may speak Your word, by stretching out Your hand to heal, and that signs and wonders may be done through the name of Your holy Servant Jesus. And when they had prayed, the place where they were assembled together was shaken; and they were all filled with the Holy Spirit, and they spoke the word of God with boldness (Acts 4:23-31).

Faced with powers they simply could not resist, this group didn't file a grievance with City Hall nor did they fire up an email blast. They had nothing and no one to turn to. We could learn a great lesson here. When faced with such dire circumstances, they went with nothing into His presence and came out with fresh fire. Confronted by inequity and persecution, they rejoiced—and they overcame!

Something else we might discover we need more of is *reaching*. We must become more effective at reaching people for Christ.

Say all you want about the move of the Holy Spirit in church today; but if such an outpouring isn't driving us to reach hurting people, it really is frighteningly similar to Paul's "sounding brass or a clanging cymbal" (1 Cor. 13:1). Performance without power will stimulate the natural man, and can fill a building with people if done with excellence. But such shallow machinations by men will not produce change and break the bonds of the Enemy.

Juxtapose these two ideas and draw your own conclusions. First, consider what Jesus said about the purpose and production of the Holy Spirit: "But you shall receive power when the Holy Spirit has come upon you; and you shall be witnesses to Me in Jerusalem, and in all Judea and Samaria, and to the end of the earth" (Acts 1:8).

The coming of the Holy Spirit propels us to be witnesses, to lay down our lives, as it were, to share the story of His redemptive plan. That's one side of this equation. Here's the other: Virtually 99 percent of the church population in America never brings one person to Christ. While that can be attributed, by some, to not possessing the gift of evangelism, the sad part is that almost 90 percent of us never even invite anyone to attend church with us.

You decide. Jesus said the outpouring of the Holy Spirit was going to propel us to become *witnesses*. Actually, the word Jesus used is the one from which we derive the term *martyr*, so it's not a stretch to say the Holy Spirit is given to enable us to lay down our lives for Christ. Yet only about one in ten in the American church will even invite someone to come to church with us. Can you still, with integrity, assert we don't need MORE of God today?

Finally, let's explore, for a moment, the idea of *release*. You do understand that Jesus wants us to be free, don't you? "Therefore if the Son makes you free, you shall be free indeed" (John 8:36).

Everything I read about Jesus involved Him setting someone free. If you read through the Gospels, you will discover Jesus either going to or coming from setting someone free. His simple statement bears out this fact; He wants us to be free—totally, completely, entirely free.

When we hear such things today, we get excited and whip up a case of religious fervor. We are, according to one older chorus, going to go down to our Enemy's camp, raid the place, and take back all he stole from us. That's exciting. I've seen us become almost frantic about all we are going to do.

Then, reality hits. The emotional eruption past . . . the energy of the crowd abated, large portions of the church are so bound they can't even lift their hands and offer God praise! We can utter the words of Jesus about being free, and even create a little buzz in the church over freedom; but it has been my experience that the whole time we have shouted over our freedom we still leave bound tightly by things such as religion, bad attitudes, and selfish motives. Millions of American Christians are bound by unforgiveness. Hurts from the past still hold them as tightly as any chain made by man. We dare not venture into the addictions that plague us. Don't you find it interesting that in church we rail at the addictions which aren't ours and cringe or defiantly excuse ourselves when our problems come to light? I am in no way advocating a "cleaning house" movement in the church. What I long for is a visitation of His Spirit, for MORE of His glory, so that we can become broken vessels in His presence and be released from the junk holding us back. Then, and only then, will we be able to penetrate the spiritual darkness that hangs around us like a belligerent fog and witness the power of God being released on hurting humanity. May God find us hungry for MORE in a time of outpouring!

A. W. Tozer is credited with saying God would take nine steps to meet us, but that last one—or first one, depending on your interpretation—was up to us. God has taken nine steps. He has invited us to come for MORE of Him today. The rest is up to us. May He discover in us a willing body, hungry for MORE of His glory, that we might be changed and witness His power to change others.

Chapter 2

THERE IS MORE AVAILABLE

Ask the Lord for rain in the time of the latter rain. The Lord will make flashing clouds; He will give them showers of rain, grass in the field for everyone (Zech. 10:1).

It is one thing to say we need more as a motivation to stretch ourselves. It is an entirely different affair to realize how much more is available, how much more God wants to give us. Perhaps the most pressing reason we can list for a refusal to settle for what we have is the fact so much more is available.

Can any among us say with an ounce of integrity we have exhausted the limitless bounty of our incomprehensible God? Is it possible our problem lies in the fact we have bought into the stubborn lie from Satan that we have exhausted God's patience, gone too far, or that He has written us off? That simply *cannot* be the case! As I understand God, based on His revelation of Himself to us, there is so much more of His glory available to us we have barely scratched the surface.

Yes, we have failed, veered off course, chosen the wrong things. In short, we have sinned in many ways. I know that is difficult for us to acknowledge, but since revival is all about getting "real" with God, let's not play word games. Today's church has fallen into a state of disrepair similar to the walls of Nehemiah's day, and nothing short of broken repentance will bring the restoration of God's Spirit we so desperately need.

We needn't be afraid of coming to God, asking for more, when we haven't been up to par ourselves. God won't turn us away. He won't send smoking flames from heaven to consume us. No! He will receive us and turn our lives around. Sure, there are those writing off the church, telling us how God has moved on. How can that be the case when the Lord has sent us words such as these? "Through the Lord's mercies we are not consumed, because His compassions fail not. They are new every morning; great is Your faithfulness" (Lam. 3:22-23).

Could it be possible that we (the church) have been duped by Satan (the big liar) and his mouthpiece (judgmental culture)? Is it possible we have allowed the world's negativity to invade our thinking and cause us to believe God has deserted us because we haven't always gotten it right?

Think about it . . . that's exactly what the world tells us, and what religion tells us. Those two strange bedfellows will combine and hammer the inconsistency of a believer. They will tag-team and berate a struggling pastor. They join forces and belittle the church that seeks for a move of God. If their doggerel is left unchecked and unbattled by the true Word of God, it will cause us to shrink back, to actually believe God is no longer interested in us. May such scatological nonsense be laid permanently to rest!

Remember this: *The MORE you and I need isn't coming from a hypocritical culture or a dead religious system; it's coming from the God who bids us come to Him—imperfect, broken, hurting—and He will provide the answers we need!* Religion, pharisaical people, and the current crop of "naysayers" who seem to be on every corner will always be more than ready to write off the church, to denounce any attempt to seek for a real move of God. You and I must always keep this uppermost in our minds as we combat their negativity. Our help isn't coming from them; it is coming from the One who bids us to seek for MORE!

A Sovereign Move of God

While there is no doubt there have been seasons where God moved in powerful and unexplained ways, it is taking the lazy man's way out to sit back and blame our lack of success on God. Sure, there have been the more recognizable seasons of outpouring in recent years: Brownsville, Toronto, Kansas City, to name a few. Usually we designate those as "sovereign moves of God." It is also true that smaller venues, or local churches, have witnessed powerful outpourings resulting in people coming to Christ, great healings, mighty outpourings of the Spirit. If you listen to some describe those events, you will no doubt hear them called "sovereign moves of God." Most times that expression is tainted with a bit of resignation that God is doing something for them He has no intention of doing for us.

I do believe God is sovereign and can do anything He desires. After all, He is God. And yes, it does seem God selects certain places and seasons for a dramatic outpouring of His glory. Still, I can't escape from the promise God placed squarely in our lap. For instance, revisit this familiar passage: "If My people who are called by My name will humble themselves, and pray and seek My face, and turn from their wicked ways, then I will hear from heaven, and will forgive their sin and heal their land" (2 Chron. 7:14).

There is nothing about sovereignty there. There is nothing selective there. Far from being exclusionary, that single verse sets us all up as potential recipients of a powerful visit from God.

Some are quick to point out the Old Testament location of that promise, citing it belongs only to Israel. While I disagree with that premise—and I contend it remains a formula that today's church can employ to see God's glory—there are, nonetheless, promises located securely within the confines of the New Testament that reveal to us the desire of God to make Himself known to every one of His children.

For instance, listen to a segment of the first sermon preached after Pentecost had rocked Jerusalem: "Repent therefore and be converted, that your sins may be blotted out, so that times of refreshing may come from the presence of the Lord" (Acts 3:19).

Repentance on our part, according to the Spirit-filled apostle, will bring two things. First, our sins will be erased. That fact alone should cause such rejoicing, such tumultuous praise, to rise up in the church that it would resemble any revival on record!

Second—and this is the area I wish to focus on most of all—repentance will bring "seasons of refreshing." This phrase is interesting because it is the only time this particular word is used in the New Testament. It carries the idea of a refreshing wind, a renewal of strength.

A kindred verb is used by Jesus: "Because lawlessness will abound, the love of many will grow cold" (Matt. 24:12). Jesus warned us things were going to get so tough, times were going to become so dangerous, and events in the last days were going to be so hard on people that many were going to allow their love for God, their ardor for things of the Spirit, to grow cold, or weary. In other words, the exact opposite of what will happen when we come to God with utter repentance.

Many among us are swift to point out the demise of the American church. We have allowed Matthew 24:12 to become part of our lifestyle. Entire religious industries have been created to staunch the bleeding. Leaders are wringing their hands, and pastors are wondering what is going to happen. "How can we turn this thing around?" seems to be the question foremost on the mind of many church leaders. Yet the whole time we have been lamenting our situation and searching for answers, the simple solution has been right under our nose! The answer we so desperately need is a *refreshing wind* of the Holy Spirit, and *repentance* is the action that will bring Him powerfully into our midst.

That is precisely the message Jesus was attempting to communicate to the Laodicean church: "Behold, I stand at the door and knock. If anyone hears My voice and opens the door, I will come in to him and dine with him, and he with Me" (Rev. 3:20).

In short, Jesus told them He was right outside, just waiting on them to make Him welcome. His message was, and is, so simple and so profound that most of us miss it. When we decide to make room for Him in our lives, our finances, our marriages, and our church services, He will show up and provide us with more than enough of what we need to take care of all our problems. He is simply waiting on some people to get serious, to truly repent and make Him first in their lives. He will rush in and provide the rest.

On the Outside Looking In

Many of us in the Western church have a poster boy in the New Testament. His story is an oft-overlooked saga, couched in one of the most beloved stories Jesus ever told.

> "Now his older son was in the field. And as he came and drew near to the house, he heard music and dancing. So he called one of the servants and asked what these things meant. And he said to him, 'Your brother has come, and because he has received him safe and sound, your father has killed the fatted calf.' But he was angry and would not go in. Therefore his father came out and pleaded with him. So he answered and said to his father, 'Lo, these many years I have been serving you; I never transgressed your commandment at any time; and yet you never gave me a young goat, that I might make merry with my friends. But as soon as this son of yours came, who has devoured your livelihood with harlots, you killed the fatted calf for him.' And he said to him, 'Son, you are always with me, and all that I have is yours'" (Luke 15:25-31).

Thousands of volumes have been written about the Prodigal Son. The number of sermons preached about this lad would probably reach into the millions. No wonder... he touches something deep within us all. We can readily, if we are willing to admit such, identify with the boy. We know the pain of wasting time, squandering resources, as well as the gracious "welcome back home."

However, it's not the glorious return of the Prodigal Son that buzzes in my mind just now. Rather, I want to look past the welcome party—beyond the glitz and glamour of a wealthy and powerful father lavishing upon an undeserving son gifts of grace and mercy. Let us look further, past the celebration, out to a hot and dirty field. Out there, laboring in the scalding sun, drenched in sweat, caked with mud from the mingling perspiration and swirling dust, there's another son—strong-willed, stalwart, tough. Disciplined in the ways of duty and perseverance, this kid can take whatever life throws at him. Day by wearying day, he completes his never-ending tasks. He comes home from a grueling day of intense labor, eats a meal, and then sinks deeper and deeper into a sense of loneliness and mediocrity. I've often wondered if this boy's heart didn't follow his younger brother when he left for a life of worldly living.

He elicits in me a very similar vein of thinking I see in today's church. For years these individuals have faithfully taught the class, counted the money, and cleaned the restrooms. They have diligently sung the songs, preached the sermons, buried the dead, and married the young. Year after year, they have plugged in on Sunday, done their duty, and gone home wondering why it's grown so wearying.

The ugly truth is, as long as everyone else is trudging along, doing their thing, and working hard, it is perfectly acceptable to muddle through, hang in there, and stoically do the work. But when some Johnny-come-lately who has not paid the price everyone else has paid shows up and the Father starts lavishing blessing after blessing on his life, that's a different story! Suddenly, doing the work, carrying the load, wearily trudging through month after month of just getting by doesn't seem fair.

That, my friend, is precisely what is pictured in the story Jesus told. The older brother spent day after day, working like a fool, grinding himself, and laboring like a slave. Suddenly, up pops the younger son ("wonder kid") who has done everything possible to embarrass his father. He has lived like a fool. He has wasted time, squandered resources, taken talent and ability and treated them like trash. Then, the moment he tops the hill—the second he crosses the horizon—the father pours on him such lavish treatment and blesses him with such royal bounty, it is as if that wandering son is the only possession the Father has left.

That is the proverbial straw that broke the older son's back. It was more than he could take. That is the very scenario being played out in tens of thousands of American churches today!

- "What's wrong? We've been here for years, grinding things out, keeping the doors open and the bills paid for the last three decades . . . and they pop in here, start some new thing, and they can't accommodate the people!"

- "I just don't get it! I've been teaching this class for fifteen years, grinding away . . . and he's been saved less than a year and they flock to him like he is Paul reincarnate!"
- "Something is wrong! I took my children to church all their lives . . . made them go to Sunday school . . . chose Vacation Bible School over real vacation. Now they won't darken the doors of a church, and last week three drug-addicted teens were delivered in a service!"
- "I've been here forty years . . . taken care of just about every job in church there is. The truth is, if it weren't for me and a couple more like me, this church wouldn't even be here. I haven't sensed God in decades. Now this new bunch pops in off the street and is filled with the joy of the Lord, or something. Makes me mad!"

This strikes close to home, doesn't it? Here's the hidden truth we who have been in church a long time don't want anyone to know: *It irritates the daylights out of us when the Father gives them what we refuse to access!*

Study any move of God and you will discover a very disheartening fact: The group that puts the most pressure on the newly revived is the group that was formerly the recipient of revival. Watch closely and see if the most ardent critics of worship are former worshipers. Listen very carefully and you will uncover the fact that the most vocal critics of revival are the formerly revived. Guess who has the most negative criticism of a growing church— it is always a church in decline. It drives us crazy when the Father starts giving *them* what He has made available to us, but we won't do anything with it. That's why the church is rife with sarcasm and bitterness. This explains, to a great extent, why we war with each other and can't stand to celebrate the success of someone else. It's tearing us apart that they have it, and we don't!

Perhaps it is time some of us come face-to-face with some sobering facts. First, we have to realize our Father will never make us access what He has for us. Remember, the whole time that younger brother was out living a wild life while the older brother was working hard to keep things going, the older brother could have had an opulent party anytime he wanted. Had he ever said to his father, "I think this weekend I am going to host a party for some of my friends—do you mind if we have a great beef roast?" the answer from the father would have been a resounding "Yes!" Sadly, this boy never took advantage of all that was rightfully his.

God will never make us take anything from Him. If you are a pastor and you don't want an outpouring in your church that disrupts your plans, don't worry . . . God won't force you to take it, even though it is available. Are you a believer who is adamant you aren't going to receive anything from God that smacks of the supernatural, which might cause you to look "foolish" to your friends? Put that fear to bed. Even though there are depths of the Spirit that you have never plumbed, God won't make you go there. Even though God has more than we will ever need, and promised time and time again to be with us and supply every need in our lives, He isn't going to force us to take the necessary steps to receive such blessing. He will allow us to labor along in our own strength for as long as we wish.

Second—and this is the really scary part—God will take what was intended for us and give it to someone else if we refuse to access His blessing. Remember what the father told that pouting older brother? "Son, you are always with me, and all that I have is yours" (Luke 15:31).

The calf the younger brother received was the property of the older brother. The robe put on that scoundrel's back was taken from the older brother's closet. The ring on his finger was sized for the older brother. Those new shoes put on the dirty feet of the wasteful boy . . . you got it—they were made for the older brother. Everything the father owned was the property of that hardworking, nose-to-the-grindstone, keep-things-going-at-all-costs older brother. But, since he wasn't going to use it, the father gave it away!

This scene scares the daylights out of me! It takes me to a statement Jesus made which, on the surface, doesn't seem equitable at all: "Therefore consider carefully how you listen. Whoever has will be given more; whoever does not have, even what he thinks he has will be taken from him" (8:18 NIV).

We in the American church need to wake up and realize God is not ruled by the same liberal mind-set that seems to dominate our landscape. He doesn't operate the same way we choose to govern ourselves. If someone in today's America doesn't have much and isn't driven to produce, we take care of them, at least to some extent. We offer government programs to enhance the little they have. We offer opportunities for a better life. Should someone accept the challenge and raise themselves up, we celebrate. However, if people decide to live on bare subsistence means, we have decided through welfare and other programs to sustain their lifestyle.

While we think that is the "Christlike" thing to do, and on many levels it is, God has clearly shown His church through this story and by what He said that He isn't going to act in the same manner. If we are going to act like the elder brother in the story Jesus told, He will take what is rightfully ours and lavish it on whoever will receive, even if they have been less than upright in their conduct. This frightens me! We in the church, particularly those of us in the Pentecostal movements, have had at our disposal blessing and power for generations. Rather than walking in His glory, we seem content to simply get by, keep the machinery running, and prop ourselves up with often-inflated numbers. And, make no mistake about this, we will fire salvo after salvo at anyone who isn't of our exact tribe who seems to be gaining ground in God!

Remember, God makes promises—and He will see them through. Rest assured that in these dark days, individuals will experience a mighty move of God; it cannot be avoided!

> "It shall come to pass in the last days, says God, that I will pour out of My Spirit on all flesh; your sons and your daughters shall prophesy, your young men shall see visions, your old men shall dream dreams. And on My menservants and on My maidservants I will pour out My Spirit in those days; and they shall prophesy" (Acts 2:17-18).

Someone's children, some church's youth group, some gathering of hungry young adults somewhere *are* going to experience a mighty outpouring of the Holy Spirit. The Spirit of God *is* going to visit the lives of people around this planet in the last days. MORE is coming to someone. I want those people to be my children . . . my grandchildren. I want those churches to be my churches.

Consider this promise: "It shall come to pass that whoever calls on the name of the Lord shall be saved" (v. 21).

Someone *is* going to be saved. Someone, somewhere, *is* going to be convicted by the Holy Spirit as MORE of God becomes the norm in a locale. They are going to call on the name of the Lord and be saved. That's not just a possibility but a firm reality when He shows up. Why can't the place where He flows freely, resulting in massive waves of people being swept into the kingdom of God, be here . . . now?

Another promise is this: "You shall receive power when the Holy Spirit has come upon you; and you shall be witnesses to Me in Jerusalem, and in all Judea and Samaria, and to the end of the earth" (1:8).

There will come a time when some group is going to have such a powerful visitation of the Spirit—when so much MORE of God is going to be revealed in their lives—that they are no longer going to be content with uttering a few phrases in an unknown tongue. Just having a good "bless me" service won't cut it any longer. No, He is going to pour out so much MORE that this group is going to stagger out like drunk people and fearlessly carry the message of Christ and His power to set men and women free.

Make no mistake, this is happening today. Known only to God, there are groups of men and women who have tasted MORE and are ready to die for the sake of Christ. Indeed, some are dying . . . miracles are transpiring . . . waves of souls are being won. We must refuse to settle for the "elder-brother syndrome" and must not belittle those whom God is blessing. We should find the place where MORE is available for our lives as well.

Chapter 3

INTOXICATING POWER

Ask the Lord for rain in the time of the latter rain. The Lord will make flashing clouds; He will give them showers of rain, grass in the field for everyone. For the idols speak delusion; the diviners envision lies, and tell false dreams; they comfort in vain. Therefore the people wend their way like sheep; they are in trouble because there is no shepherd. "My anger is kindled against the shepherds, and I will punish the goatherds. For the Lord of hosts will visit His flock, the house of Judah, and will make them as His royal horse in the battle." . . . Those of Ephraim shall be like a mighty man, and their heart shall rejoice as if with wine. Yes, their children shall see it and be glad; their heart shall rejoice in the Lord" (Zech. 10:1-3, 7).

How many times have we used the Old Testament to beat up struggling souls? We pick out a prophet and then preach him like we and God are angry, and sometimes we are. While God is angry in this passage, His vile is not directed at the struggling sheep of His pasture. Rather, it is channeled at the leaders who had been instrumental in leading the people astray. As for the wandering sheep, God had every intention of demonstrating powerful change in their lives.

This is borne out in Paul's language to the Romans: "For whatever things were written before were written for our learning, that we through the patience and comfort of the Scriptures might have hope" (15:4).

These words bring us hope—not condemnation because of the position we happen to occupy at the moment, but hope that God will visit us and bring radical change to our lives. Those of Ephraim who were going to rejoice were the marginalized, forgotten, defeated people of the northern ten tribes that had already fallen captive. They had been pushed to the edges by circumstance. Listening to false teachers who promised nothing but sunny skies, they walked down a path that led to destruction. But God wasn't through with them. He was going to visit them again and change their lives. In spite of how bad things happened to be at the moment, they had hope!

If you find yourself today locked into something hopeless, something from which you cannot extract yourself, God has a message of hope. Even if you walked blindly after some false promise, believing what you were told, and find youself locked into something from which you can never imagine yourself being free, God sends you a message of hope. He will come and work a mighty miracle in your life!

The Flow of New Wine

Zechariah spoke of something happening—something profound. He talked about hopeless people rejoicing like they were drunk on wine—depressed, marginalized people rejoicing like a banquet where wine was freely flowing. Don't make the mistake the world makes of seeing this image and assuming he was talking about a drunken debacle, where everyone gets so inebriated they forget for a while their problems and then sober up, only to face the same situations as before, and now with a headache. No, he was talking about the intoxicating presence of the Holy Spirit. Throughout the Old Testament, wine is a symbol of the ministry of the Holy Spirit. This reference is no different.

Our Father wants to visit us with a fresh outpouring of the wine of the Holy Spirit. While He is moving like liquid fire around the rest of the world, our Father wants us to be equally filled to intoxication with the glory of the Holy Spirit.

Everyone reading this is well acquainted with the tragedy of too much wine. Drunkenness ensues, and disaster soon follows. Consider the following facts:

- May 14, 1988 . . . A man driving drunk in Carroll County, Kentucky, crossed the median of the interstate and struck a church bus head-on. Fire engulfed the wreckage, killing twenty-seven innocent people and severely injuring thirty-four others.
- In Ness City, Kansas, a small town with just over twenty-nine hundred residents, catastrophe gripped the entire village as three teens were killed in four weeks, all driving drunk.
- Untreated addiction is more expensive than three of the nation's top ten killers. It is six times more expensive than heart disease, which costs over $133 billion per year. It outstrips diabetes, which costs $130 billion per year. It is four times more expensive than cancer, which costs $96 billion per year.
- Every American adult pays nearly $1,000 per year for the damages of addiction.
- Alcohol contributes to 100,000 deaths annually, making it the third leading cause of preventable mortality in the United States.
- Forty percent of all traffic fatalities are alcohol-related.
- Of those who die in fires, between 48 and 64 percent are intoxicated.
- Alcohol is involved in 86 percent of homicides, 60 percent of sexual offenses, 37 percent of assaults, and 13 percent of child-abuse cases.
- Fully one quarter of all emergency room admissions are due to alcohol.

The list could go on and on. In spite of the obvious, this is not a temperance lecture. Rather, this is a call for all-out, complete, utter immersion in "wine." The difference is, we need a fresh refilling of the wine Paul mentioned—the Holy Spirit: "And do not be drunk with wine, in which is dissipation; but be filled with the Spirit" (Eph. 5:18).

What we seem to have missed in our efforts to make sure people stay away from intoxication, as well we should, is the need for MORE of His Spirit in our own lives. Understand, as horrific as *too much natural wine* is, so too is the presence of *too little wine of the Holy Spirit* in the church! It is not difficult at all to recount story after gut-wrenching story of the catastrophes caused by someone who had too much to drink. It is not difficult either to recount story after story of the sad results of those lost from the Kingdom because we did not have enough of the Spirit's presence.

In no way do I seek to diminish the pain and agony suffered by loved ones who have endured the tragic losses caused by alcohol. Words cannot describe the depth of grief that encircles those who have been informed they will never see a loved one again simply because someone had "too much to drink." But when one looks beyond the natural, into the spiritual, and notices the thousands of churches that close their doors every year in America, and pays enough attention to the encroachment of Islam into the "Christian world," including the United States, an accompanying sense of loss and grief ensues.

Simply put, the church in America is dying. We are losing ground right and left in spite of all our boastings and megachurches and religious celebrities. It's time we came face-to-face with some sobering realities:

- We are not in this situation because the days are evil.
- It is not because the people just are not interested in God anymore.
- Sorry, we are not here because we are living in the last days.
- No, this has not fallen out to us because the days of revival are past.

Instead, We Have Lost the Intoxicating Power of the Spirit!

We, like the wending sheep in Zechariah's day, have fallen under the intoxicating spell of smooth-talking teachers who promise nothing but bliss and sunny days. I love the way Eugene Peterson translated part of Zechariah's prophecy: "Store-bought gods babble gibberish. Religious experts spout rubbish. They pontificate hot air. Their prescriptions are nothing but smoke. And so the people wander like lost sheep, poor lost sheep without a shepherd" (10:2 TM).

It was not an absence of religious teaching and talk that led to their demise. They, just like us, had it on every corner. It was the utter senselessness of what was being said and taught that led them to their bondage. Likewise, it takes only a few moments to catch up on today's popular religious themes to understand why we are in such desperate shape. That which is taught, and ultimately accepted, in this nation has led us to a precipice from which we will be lucky to escape.

Listen to the widely accepted teaching today: Boiled down to the essential elements, Jesus came and died a grueling death so you could rule, be in dominion, possess greater wealth and health; in other words, live a good American life! The church? It is here to please you, help you get to know your neighbor better, and never take more than seventy-five minutes of your time in a week. And whatever we do, we cannot allow any demonstration of the Holy Spirit that might cause someone to be uncomfortable, lest they never return.

We have fallen into bondage because we have listened to such gibberish. While telling us how great we are and what a tremendous job we are doing, the modern-day prophets focus on money and good times. Ignoring the deeper truths and ugly realities facing us, they are content to build their own empires on the backs of wandering sheep who hope to cash in on the false hopes they hold forth. While this has been going on, churches have been dying by the thousands every year in America. The whole time we have been mesmerized by these slick presenters of half-truths, our attendance numbers have been dwindling to the point we are no longer winning enough people to Jesus to say we are winning our own children.

This probably sounds radical, and certainly is not what you are going to hear on most Christian television programs: Jesus did not die on the cross to make you a fat, happy, sassy, prosperous American Christian. He did not give His all on that bloody hillside just so we could build bigger nest eggs and have a comfy retirement while the rest of the world lives in abject poverty. Jesus did not have the flesh stripped from His back just so you and I could endure a little less arthritic pain. No, He did not pour out the Holy Spirit at Pentecost just to enable us to have a nice little church service and head off to Sunday lunch.

He endured all that so He could raise up a group of radical zealots who would risk all, give up everything, forsake anything that stood in the way, and brazenly take on the powers of darkness which hold this world in sway. He did all that so we could flourish like horses of battle, the type mentioned here by Zechariah, rather than spend the rest of our lives wandering around like puny little lost sheep. It is not His intention that we stand over in a corner and bleat like pitiful sheep while the wolves of the Enemy pick us off one by one. He wants us to be so intoxicated and full of the wine of the Holy Spirit that we rail like men of war, declaring the power of God to set people free!

But This Is a New Day!

I understand the sentiments of many—it is a new day, a new time. The people we are trying to reach will not stand for anything that smacks of the supernatural. If they cannot have it neatly packaged, easily received, and readily disposed of upon leaving the church, they will not come back. Pastors across America live in the fear that people, particularly the heavy givers, are going to be offended by a demonstration of the Holy Spirit and leave the church. I know . . . I have lived with that same fear.

Perhaps it is time we shift our gaze away from the stony faces of men and look again at the heart of God. He wants us to be changed, filled, drunk with the wine of the Holy Spirit. Make no mistake about it—if you decide to follow His path and forsake that of men, you *will* have dissenters and deserters; it comes with the turf.

Remember, this whole thing started with an event that was unexplainable, unattractive, even undignified:

> When the Day of Pentecost had fully come, they were all with one accord in one place. And suddenly there came a sound from heaven, as of a rushing mighty wind, and it filled the whole house where they were sitting. Then there appeared to them divided tongues, as of fire, and one sat upon each of them. And they were all filled with the Holy Spirit and began to speak with other tongues, as the Spirit gave them utterance (Acts 2:1-4).

As wonderful as that moment must have been, we simply cannot stop reading at that point and begin to preach about the joys of Pentecost. Integrity demands we read on, take in the full scope of reactions that day. As hard as it was for me to accept, it was revealed to me very early the ugly fact that not everyone is going to rejoice with me or accept with gladness the news of the Spirit's arrival.

Before the echo of the roar had rattled down the Kidron Valley and vibrated out of earshot, the gossipmongers had begun their attacks. "Then they were all amazed and marveled, saying to one another, 'Look, are not all these who speak Galileans?'" (v. 7).

It was impossible, they argued, for such a vagabond group from Galilee to possess such intense language skills. Something had to be up for them to be able to exercise such eloquence.

Of course, the dismissal of a move of the Spirit, which people could not understand and did not want to happen, continued with perplexity and name-calling: "So they were all amazed and perplexed, saying to one another, 'Whatever could this mean?' Others mocking said, 'They are full of new wine'" (vv. 12-13).

All around the church today are well-fed leaders who instruct us to tone down, to shove the results of a true Pentecost into a dark corner. It is argued that the world doesn't understand the moving of the Spirit, so it must be relegated to the inner circles of the elite. It is asserted that complete and utter abandonment in the presence of the Holy Spirit elicits laughter and mockery from an unbelieving world; hence we must not have any such shameful display in public worship today. The world, as well as the passive, unbelieving church, has always misunderstood and mocked the genuine article of the Holy Spirit since the day He arrived. What's so different about our day except our inordinate fawning before the gods of numbers and acceptance?

We don't need to back down, tone down, or sit down. We need a fresh intoxication of the Holy Spirit's fire, followed by someone who will dare to stand up and point to Jesus. The church today needs a fresh drunkenness in the Spirit to say to a dying world, "Jesus has the power to change your life," and live out that change before them. That is the essential message of the church today—"Jesus saves." But we have become so docile, so embarrassed by all the "junk" done in the name of our Lord, we have shrunk into our shells and embedded ourselves in the hope Jesus comes to get us before it all gets too bad. That is not what Jesus intends His church to be!

Wandering Sheep or Warring Stallions?

The image Zechariah communicated from God is colorful. Two contrasting animals—one portraying the way things are, the other the way God intends things to be—display clearly why we need MORE of the Lord today: "For the idols speak delusion; the diviners envision lies, and tell false dreams; they comfort in vain. Therefore the people wend their way like sheep; they are in trouble because there is no shepherd. 'My anger is kindled against the shepherds, and I will punish the goatherds. For the Lord of hosts will visit His flock, the house of Judah, and will make them as His royal horse in the battle'" (Zech. 10:2-3).

Because they had listened to the babble of the false teachers, they had become much like "wandering sheep." Most of us don't know much about sheep. There are not many sheep farms in the region in which I live. However, those of us who have studied biblical language and images realize we are not being complimented very much when we are called "sheep." To be honest, sheep are not the most brilliant and self-sufficient animals on the planet.

The image used by Zechariah aptly describes the vast majority of believers in today's church:

- Gullible, easily taken in by a flashy promise
- Easily intimidated
- Distracted by the slightest circumstance

- Easy pickings for the predators of our day
- Like sheep, barely able to see beyond our own nose
- Skittish, frightened by just about anything
- Always standing around, bleating, crying, and waiting on someone to come by and save us
- Powerless to do anything about it when the Enemy shows up

Let's be honest . . . that sorry description pegs most of us to a tee! We have listened to the empty teachings of "American Christianity" until we have become soft and convinced it really is all about us and our comfort. Sacrifice is virtually unheard-of in the American church. We are intimidated to speak out about Jesus and so easily distracted by the shiny "stuff" of our lives that it is difficult for many American Christians to make it to a solid month of services in a row. We are scared to death of Islam, high gas prices, and inflation, and we are hoping against hope that the pre-Tribulation rapture happens fast!

The result is a church in America that is just holding on. It's sad, and the worst part is, it doesn't have to be that way.

Contrast the image of the wandering sheep—hopeless and helpless—with the second image. No longer wandering sheep, a man or woman who encounters the intoxicating power of the Holy Spirit will be transformed into a warring steed.

Consider the notion of being the "battle horse" for a moment. The battle horse was the choice of the mighty man or the king when armies were going to war. While some animals (e.g., sheep) are so easily frightened that the leader has to find a still pool of water for them to drink (Ps. 23:2), the battle steed hears the clash of armor and rushes headlong into the fray.

While sheep are so skittish and afraid of a place where they have previously been startled that they often had to be physically carried by the shepherd when they approached that spot, the battle steed would rush into the very places he had been wounded, burned, cut open, almost killed, and with a roar of adrenalin stand his ground and die before he gave an inch. Oh that we had MORE of Him, so much MORE that we shake off our bland acceptance of "church-as-usual" and rush headlong into the spiritual battles taking place today! May God grant us the spirit of "I will die standing my post, waiting on His glory, before I back down one inch!"

There is a true story that powerfully illustrates this point. It is about a horse named Sefton, who served in the Royal Cavalry Guard in London. He was an exceptional animal. While this service was for horses that were completely black, Sefton was so impressive he was accepted even though he had white stockings and a white blaze on his face. On July 20, 1982, Sefton was part of a royal march alongside Hyde Park. He, along with his fifteen compatriots, marched in splendid dignity. Suddenly, out of nowhere, a car exploded as twenty-five pounds of dynamite ignited. Wrapped with hundreds of four- and six-inch nails, the device set by a cowardly mongrel exploded by remote control. In a fiery flash, seven horses were killed and another eight, including Sefton, were grievously wounded.

The brave warring steed suffered multiple wounds in his neck from pieces of car metal. One two-inch-long shard severed his jugular vein. Five four-inch-long nails were implanted half their length into his face, one spiked deep into his back. His side and flanks were gored by the shrapnel from the car. His right eye deeply burned and the cornea damaged, Sefton was almost killed. So severe was his neck wound, a passerby's shirt was stuffed into the gaping hole in an attempt to staunch the bleeding. Sefton was led away to the vet, but no one expected him to survive. It took hours of surgery to repair the thirty-eight different wounds. Sefton was given a fifty-fifty chance of survival.

The amazing thing is that during the whole ordeal—with the smoke, explosions, the searing heat, and intense pain he suffered—Sefton never flinched. His rider, Trooper Pederson, himself wounded, later recounted how Sefton never bolted, never tried to throw him to the ground, and never once made an attempt to escape the hellish inferno in which he was caught. He stood his ground, as a warring steed, determined to die if need be rather than abandon his calling.

Perhaps even more amazing is the fact he survived and a few weeks later, again mounted by Trooper Pederson, Sefton strode gallantly by the very spot where his greatest battle had been fought. Never flinching, swaying, or wavering one inch, he marched right by the valley of the shadow of his own death with a strident determination to fulfill his destiny and calling. He was a warring steed, not a wandering sheep, and even death wasn't going to prevent him from doing what he was born to do! Sometime later, as the story of this warring steed became better known, he was ridden into an arena in London where thousands of Brits stood and gave a roaring applause to the mighty horse of battle which would not run but would rather die standing his ground before he backed down.

Surely that is precisely what God wants to make every one of us. He wants to revolutionize us, make us so intoxicated with His Spirit that we are transformed people who, instead of running and hiding from the advances of the Enemy, wade into it. When we hear of a need, we rush toward it. When we sense injustice, we stand for the powerless. When we see the trampling of the poor, we refuse to go to our comfortable homes and sit in our comfortable churches and ignore their plight. Instead, we roar like lions of heaven and call for the glory of God to be manifested in the earth.

God is certainly shaking us in America—particularly the American church—to arouse us to have MORE of Him so our nice, neatly prescribed little church services where our pet needs are addressed for the hundredth time are no longer the norm. In place of that will come times of travail and ensuing power where the back of Satan is broken in the lives of people and they are set free! No longer will we sit around and worry about what someone says or thinks about us. Instead, there will be a dogged determination to run like a horse of war to the sound of the revealed glory of God in the lives of worshipers. How different it would be in the American church if—instead of having us sitting around, whining about the way things are, pouting because someone did not treat us the way we thought we should have been treated, lamenting our forever-lost golden past—we were suddenly filled with tens of thousands of men and women of valor and war who faced the enemy of our souls and declared, "The Lord is against you!" Such a revival would sweep this nation it would defy description! May we become so intoxicated—so drunk in Him—we refuse to continue to just go along, allowing the Enemy, our fears, and our circumstances to push us around. May we become warring steeds rather than wandering sheep!

What Will This Look Like?

A question I ponder is, *What does a real move of God look like?* Equally interesting to me is the question, *What can I expect if God really shows up?* Those are legitimate questions, and you can be sure of this: a move of God is going to be a strange thing to most people. By and large, we in the church have become so carnal, so intent on pleasing people, that we have shoved God to the periphery. We are determined we are going to be in complete control, which in and of itself may explain to a great extent the absence of God's glory in most worship services. However—and mark this well—bizarre behavior by some people claiming the presence of God is not an indicator of His presence. While a genuine move of God—the outpouring of MORE of His glory mentioned by Zechariah—will produce some reactions in people that many consider strange, the real proof that God has been among us is what happens when the dust settles and we start living out what God has promised.

Take, for instance, the literal fulfillment of the prophetic word before us. Those who had come back from captivity were discouraged because many of their fellow citizens simply did not want to leave the confines of comfort and come home with them. Once they arrived, things did not pan out exactly as they had hoped. A small gathering of those who wanted to worship Jehovah in Jerusalem had assembled, and they were immediately met with intense pressure and persecution. While the adversity was unrelenting, God was up to something. History reveals the response to this tension was the formulation of a "small-group ministry" called the *synagogue*. All they needed for worship was a room and some Old Testament scriptures. The more detailed worship of the Temple might, or might not, take place. The smaller, more intimate and personal forms of worship kept them as an entity through centuries of persecution.

Later, Alexander the Great conquered the Middle East. When he approached, the high priest of Jerusalem made him welcome.

In subsequent wars, the nation fell under the rule of the Egyptian Ptolemies. It has been discovered that, in years following the Egyptian dominance of the Middle East, great Jewish communities flourished in Alexandria. So enmeshed into Egyptian society were these Jewish communities that they adopted the Greek language as their official tongue. Later, they were responsible for commissioning the first Bible translation—the Old Testament into Greek, a document we call the Septuagint (LXX).

Later, as is always the case, the Egyptians were uprooted and replaced by the infamous Antiochus Epiphanes. He named himself such because that name means "God revealed." Arrogant, full of himself, Antiochus ordered a statue of Zeus, the head god of the Greeks, to be erected over the Holy Place and sacrifices to be offered. Of course, that led to great revolt and much bloodshed. In time, a leader among the "wandering sheep" named Judas Maccabaeus arose and led a revolt that resulted in the Temple being cleansed of Greek abomination. This is celebrated each year in the Jewish holiday Hanukah.

In 63 BC, Pompey took Jerusalem for the Romans, and history slid quickly downhill from there. They slaughtered all the priests they could find at the base of the altar. In time, the Roman general Titus came and basically leveled the nation.

From the natural perspective, it was over. The people, their Temple, their home, their history, their religion . . . gone—obliterated right before their eyes. Still, in the midst of all the chaos and confusion, the death and destruction, there was this looming promise: God was going to visit them and transform them from *wandering sheep* into *warring steeds*. How? When? Where?

Tradition holds that during one particularly bitter season when Titus was causing Jewish blood to run like a river, a young rabbi named Johanan ben Zakkai was smuggled out of Jerusalem in a coffin. Supposedly, this young rabbi came upon the presence of the great Titus. He prophesied to the bloody general that he would one day inhabit the seat of power—he would be emperor of Rome. This appealed to the ego of the great military madman, so he granted the young rabbi a wish. Zakkai would be allowed to establish a small rabbinical school. From this tiny, miniscule decision began a powerful movement in Jewish history.

It is from these institutions called *yeshivot* that Jewish scholars, historians, lawyers, philosophers—all essential parts of keeping the name of Jehovah before the Jewish people—have come. These laborers have made it possible for a Jewish believer to hold tightly to Jehovah and put down roots regardless of how alien the soil beneath their feet might have been.

Of course, matters grew worse. The last stronghold against Rome was Masada. Nearly one thousand people held out there as long as they could. When it was evident they were going under, they decided upon a horrible plan. Each man was to love on his wife and children, then kill them. In turn, each man was to then lie down beside his slain family and wait for his throat to be slit by one of the ten men selected for that gruesome task. The ten then drew lots to see who would die next. The final survivor would then take his own life, the only suicide in the group.

This was basically the "curtain call" for God's people. For centuries they were scattered, forced to wander. Persecuted, killed by so-called Christian mobs, slaughtered in Inquisitions, and finally suffering under Hitler's "final solution," the Jewish people, whom God said He was going to visit and transform, seemed all but lost, abandoned, and alone.

Then, something happened. The Jewish people, who had been harried and killed like vermin, suddenly reappeared. The Nazis had sought to exterminate them. The world of Islam launched every effort to drive them into the sea. But something happened—out of nowhere! A nation was born in a day, and despite the efforts of most of the world to abort the process, Israel was once again on the world stage. In the darkness, behind closed doors, and out of the observance of most of the brilliant men of the world, God had visited His people and worked a powerful transformation. No longer were they wandering sheep, crying out for the help of anyone who might listen. Suddenly, almost overnight, they became warring steeds who would stand up gallantly to any adversary.

Think about it: in the space of a few decades, Israel has gone from hiding in crawl spaces and attics to one of the superpowers on this planet! As a matter of fact, some will even go so far as to assert the state of Israel is *the* superpower in the region of the Middle East, not the United States. Consider these startling facts:

- Israel can put to field nineteen divisions of ground troops; the United States only possesses thirteen, and it would take a long time to get large quantities on site there.
- Israel, using souped-up fighters obtained from the U.S., can put up three thousand sorties per day, while the United States can only sustain about sixteen hundred per day.
- The real difference-maker is nuclear weapons. While there is no official acknowledgment that Israel even possesses a nuclear arsenal, the worst-kept secret in military history is that this tiny nation has somewhere between sixty-five and eighty-five weapons in inventory.

Ponder the amazing facts for a second: A tiny nation of people—shoved down, slapped around, bordering on extinction for centuries, almost eliminated by the Nazis—today is one of the largest nuclear powers on the planet!

What happened? What can possibly account for such a rapid and dramatic turnaround? The answer is found in one place. As Zechariah prophesied so long ago, God did indeed visit His wandering sheep and transformed them into warring steeds.

Here's the wonderful part: As the apostle Paul told us, we have been given this glorious history to inspire hope in our lives. You and I can be confident today that our God is going to visit us and work the same spiritual transformation in our lives He has done in the natural through Israel. We can expect to experience the intoxicating visitation of the Holy Spirit when we open our hearts completely to Him. Individuals, haunted by demons of the past, afraid to take a stand lest they fall one more time, will discover themselves imbued with such boldness, overcome with such determination that they will become roaring lions of God's glory. Churches—long museums which have done little more than keep the relics of the past in good shape—will suddenly become ablaze with such dramatic worship and power they will be transformed into overcrowded nurseries that are doing their best to house and train the mighty harvest God has brought into His fold. It can happen! It has happened in the natural in Israel, and we can see it take place in the spiritual in His church today.

Chapter 4

WHAT CAN I EXPECT?

Those of Ephraim shall be like a mighty man, and their heart shall rejoice as if with wine. Yes, their children shall see it and be glad; their heart shall rejoice in the Lord (Zech. 10:7).

One of the dividing arguments in the church today is the question, "What does a real move of God look like?" As mentioned earlier, we all want to know what the genuine article looks or feels like. None of us wants to be snookered, or taken in by charlatanism. That, in great part, was what led the people of Zechariah's day to be in the predicament in which they found themselves. In our day, where there is virtually zero accountability for what one says or does, it is prudent to measure anything that calls itself, or anyone calling themselves, "of God" against a solid biblical measuring rod. Too many competing voices are pressing to be heard in today's church market for one to assume that what is being said (or what appears to be happening) is genuine for us to sit back and continue to take things at face value. We have all endured the embarrassments and gone through the disappointments of man's manipulative ways being exposed as they sought to merchandise God's treasures for man's riches. There have been too many extravagant appeals for money that was supposedly used for reaching the masses when a large portion was used to support a lavish lifestyle of the man or woman who was preaching about One who gave all. We have had enough hidden earbuds where the written ailments of desperate people have been whispered via a small intercom so the amazement of the onlookers could be aroused. It is time we dismiss as our barometer of truth how we feel about someone or how their "ministry" appeals to us. Instead, it is time we turn back once more to the rock-solid examples and teaching of Scripture. It is only there that we will find solid ground on which to rest our faith. And, as much as it is painful for us as Pentecostals to say, if the practices we are clinging to with all our might are not found squarely in God's Word, we need to abandon them like the sinking *Titanic* and move on to fashion ourselves after God's pattern!

It is here, in Zechariah's prophecy, that we can find several evidences of a genuine move of God. Call it *revival, renewal, a move of God* . . . whatever term you choose, the outcome will always be the same. When God shows up, these things are going to happen!

Rejoicing

Previously, we looked at the idea of intoxicating joy. When God gives us MORE, we are going to react in a manner somewhat similar to drunken men.

In truth, there are two differing words rendered "rejoice" in Zechariah 10:7. The first word, the one used to describe the reaction of those of us with a few more birthdays, gives us the idea of cheering up, becoming gleeful, acting a little giddy. The second word—used to describe the reactions of those who are younger, more limber, and less arthritic than we older folk—carries the idea of spinning around, jumping up and down, being delighted.

The fact of these two different words struck me. Apart from the fact of the encroachment of age, why would there be a choice of two words? After all, if you believe the Holy Spirit inspired and guided the word selection (as I do), one cannot simply overlook such things. We all know age brings deterioration of our physical abilities. Our bones, joints, even our hearts, simply cannot support the extreme physical actions we once took easily in stride. If you live long enough, you will witness people who once rejoiced in great dexterity now slow down. Perhaps they once jumped for joy before the Lord—a perfectly biblical reaction. Now, knee joints won't permit such an exercise. Throughout my life, I have known people who would dance before the Lord with abandon—as David did—but now are more sedate and reserved. Their fervor hasn't dimmed; it's a matter of their heart no longer being able to sustain the physical demands such an act of worship calls for.

As I thought about this passage, my mind wandered back a number of years to a particular camp meeting service of which I was a part as a teen. Singing in a choir, I was positioned where I had a great vantage point of the entire tabernacle. Those of my generation, as well as the preceding generations, probably have some memories evoked by the very mention of those terms. We would meet for a week, or longer, and have numerous services throughout the day. On top of that, we had them outside in the summer with no air-conditioning and dressed in suits and ties! But my, what moves of God we experienced!

One particular incident I recall involved a young man with fiery-red hair. I did not know him then, nor do I now. It was in the midst of great rejoicing that this young man decided he would run for joy—again, a perfectly biblical action (see Acts 3:8). I could trace his steps as he trekked around the outer edge of the tabernacle in which we were worshiping. I watched him make a complete lap. Somewhere along the way, he decided if one lap was good, two were better. He continued his jog (I would guess one lap equaled about four hundred yards); only the end of the second lap brought a startling reality to this man's mind. As he was gasping for air, I could almost see the little cartoon blur above his head stating, "Though He slay me, yet I will serve Him" (see Job 13:15). His body told him he might want one more lap, but it was not going to happen. Physical realities simply caught up with him, as it happens to all of us.

Yet I contend there is more here than just tight ligaments and clogged arteries. We can see a progression that has taken place in many of our lives. Incidentally, it is one that will cause us to miss out on some great things from God if we are not careful.

Honesty demands we admit that the older we get, the more experienced we become, and the more we tend to develop a tendency to corral our emotions and instead look past what is taking place right before us and look for the "next thing." Years ago, a gracious church I pastored gave my family and me a wonderful Pastor Appreciation gift. They presented us with a glorious package of a week at Disney World. I thought it was great, and it was. My sons were young at the time, and they thought it was the grandest thing on the planet. They were ecstatic, to say the least. I was happy, thrilled, and appreciative to the core. Yet my enthusiasm was tempered by the fact I knew in a few days the trip would be over and I had to come back and face the rigors of life. My sons were too young to live like that, so they had a more enthusiastic reaction than I.

I fear some of us who have been around for a while have allowed ourselves to fall into that same pattern. We have somehow stood by and not noticed as our "childish joy" in God's presence has been stolen by the pressures of life. We hate to admit it, but it is true nonetheless—far too many of us who once rejoiced with abandon in God's presence have relegated ourselves to the sidelines and become critics of those who dare to attempt what we once freely did. Call it "maturity," blame it on circumstances of life, point a finger of accusation at anyone or anything you choose . . . the bottom line is, a real move of God is going to be documented when some of us who once rejoiced before the Lord actually lighten up and regain our joy!

The natural progression of life tends to deplete the resources we have. Time not only erodes our physical abilities, but the vicissitudes of life will also sap our spiritual strength. Time and circumstance has left many a saint of God depleted, weary, and bitter. Standing after years of labor, far too many of us have little, or nothing, left in the tank.

If that describes how you feel—if you are one who stares blankly on Sunday, who goes through the motions, who is considering walking out and never coming back—I have some great news for you: MORE is headed your way, if you are willing to receive Him. Rejoicing will once more characterize your life, if you are willing to open up and follow His voice. You may not jump and run like you did as a youngster, but neither do you have to spend the rest of your journey here as an angry, bitter "used-to-be" saint who does nothing but criticize those coming behind you. You can walk in the joy of the Lord again!

Do you remember how Isaiah described the walk? "Therefore with joy you will draw water from the wells of salvation" (Isa. 12:3). Our way can be filled with joy, rejoicing!

Here's the big question: Can you be open enough to God to worship Him even though your life seems empty at the moment? Even though life has drained you of your joy, even though events have taken the edge off your ardor for God, even though you may have settled into a routine of just doing the stuff of church, a revival of joy can come your way if you are willing to sing to God while staring at nothing. Let's take a look at this in the Bible:

> From there they went to Beer, which is the well where the Lord said to Moses, "Gather the people together, and I will give them water." Then Israel sang this song: "Spring up, O well! All of you sing to it—the well the leaders sank, dug by the nation's nobles, by the lawgiver, with their staves." And from the wilderness they went to Mattanah (Num. 21:16-18).

Here we find God's people involved in God's stuff. They were on a journey to a new destination. Life, with all the trails it brings, has once more placed them in a tough spot. Involved in desert warfare, they find themselves without water. It isn't a great stretch to see a parallel between the physical and spiritual here. Like them, we get involved in life, doing all the stuff we do, and before we realize what has happened, we are depleted, dry, arid. Lacking the basic elements of the Spirit's presence, we simply run out of steam.

That's what happened to Israel. But God, our great God, always has a remedy. The Lord commanded them to dig a well. It had to be a fairly large hole. There were millions of them (including their animals) in desperate need of water, so they all dug. I love the way the Bible lets us in on small details. Moses dug, and so did the elders. They used what they had on hand—staves, sticks. It was hard, dirty, sweaty, grimy labor, but they did it!

One would think just doing the deed would be enough. After all, if we show up at church, make sure the air or heat is on, the lights are burning, the children are cared for, the ushers are ready—all the stuff it takes for a modern church to operate—that should be enough. God ought to be so impressed with our labor that He shows up in fiery glory . . . so we think!

The problem is, God has this notion that He is God and we are to operate on His system, not the other way around. Normal niceties would have dictated that at the moment they finished that hole in the ground out there in the desert, a large thunderhead would have formed over their crater and immediately filled it with millions of gallons of fresh water. Not this time . . . not with our God.

Once they had completed all their labor, God required something else—He made them sing! He called on them to rejoice, even though nothing was there. He called on them to do something they had not done since the Red Sea experience. God had His people sing to an empty hole in the ground before He filled their lives with renewing water.

Do not make the mistake of thinking that simply uttering some words, mouthing some well-known phrases, is what happened here. Oh, no! They sang with gusto and passion. As a matter of fact, this term is used to describe the *singing* done by the ladies who came out to greet David when he brought the ark back into Jerusalem (1 Sam. 18:6). This was a joyful outbreak of praise to God, which resulted in an outpouring of the very essence they so desperately needed.

The first indicator of revival in our church will certainly not be the groundswell of people being swept into the Kingdom, although that is a marker of real revival, as we shall soon see. The first thing that will take place in a genuine move of God is some of us who have been around for a while are going to rediscover the joy of our salvation. Not the joy of His blessings and His bounty, but the joy of our salvation!

Understand, that while you may be in a sticky situation today, and may be stuck facing an empty hole in life, you have the salvation of God to rejoice over. If you cannot muster joy today because of the way life has drained you, at least you can rejoice over the fact the wrath of God isn't covering you like it is with unbelievers (John 3:36). God wants you to rejoice in Him!

In spite of all our excuses, we are called upon to be people who rejoice. It is that joy which will make us strong. Sure, some of us face tough positions in life. That's why Paul told us to rejoice *in hope* (Rom. 5:2). Yes, there are those of us who have lost seemingly everything in the tough economic times we face. Again, Paul tells us to rejoice through Jesus, *because we have the reconciliation* (v. 11). No one knows my shortcomings any more than I, but I cannot allow my failures to hinder my rejoicing. The bottom line is simple: I am to rejoice all the time (Phil. 4:4)!

Let's Get Loud!

My rejoicing is to blend with your rejoicing, and we are to create a wave of joy that reaches far beyond the confines of our local church. Our rejoicing should be so boisterous and powerful that it carries far into the spiritual territory held by our Enemy.

Such was the case in one service found in the Bible. The scene was the dedication of the wall reconstructed by Nehemiah. This service took place not too long before Zechariah's day. It was a time to rejoice, to celebrate—and rejoice they did! "So the two thanksgiving choirs stood in the house of God, likewise I and the half of the rulers with me" (Neh. 12:40).

Nehemiah, as well as a large contingent of the rulers of that day, stood with not one, but two choirs, and prepared to sing to the Lord. As they lifted their voices to God, rejoicing over the goodness of the Lord, something strange started to happen: "Also that day they offered great sacrifices, and rejoiced, for God had made them rejoice with great joy; the women and the children also rejoiced, so that the joy of Jerusalem was heard afar off" (v. 43).

People started getting involved, offering sacrifices to God. Suddenly, an explosion of joy, a pandemonium of rejoicing, erupted across the entire congregation. Men, women, and children all joined in powerful celebration, rejoicing at the goodness of our God. So great, in fact, was the combined power of their rejoicing that the sound emanating from Jerusalem was heard a long way off.

Make no mistake about it—the first ripples of revival we will hear will be those of us who have done it all, seen it all, and heard it all, suddenly being refilled with glory and so much MORE of Him. No longer will we lament what used to be; no longer will we be characterized by our whines over what once was. Instead, arching far and wide, the sounds of our rejoicing over the greatness of our God will reverberate through our churches, out into our communities, and will shake our cities for God's glory. May it start today!

Chapter 5

RESTORATION

"I will whistle for them and gather them, for I will redeem them; and they shall increase as they once increased" (Zech. 10:8).

We previously noticed one of the evidences of MORE of God in our midst will be an increase in rejoicing. Who can dispute the fact that the Scripture points clearly to this phenomenon: *When God is manifest, ecstatic worship takes place!* However, there are more markers of His presence—markers equally important to rejoicing. While rejoicing can erode into a totally carnal, fleshly extravagance, these indicators of His real presence are universally undeniable.

God comes to His people for a very specific purpose. Far from displaying His presence so we might indulge in some fleshly display of emotion, God comes to touch us, change us, and transform us. He wanted Zechariah to communicate to the people in very clear terms that once He showed up, things were not going to be the same. In today's world of consumerism Christianity—where if one doesn't like the challenges being put forth at one church, all they have to do is go to another—this message isn't very popular. Indeed, very few involved in the "mass media" branch of American Christianity will bother to tell you God really wants to radically change you, but that does not deter Him from His real mission. God wants to revolutionize your life. Be careful, that can be a painful process!

Responsiveness

Part of the whole process of restoration involves our responsiveness to His voice. Pay close attention to the way God says He will call out to us: "I will whistle for them . . ." (Zech. 10:8).

The term *whistle* can easily be translated "hiss." It is something like one of us trying to get the attention of another person when we do not really want everyone else to know about it. It is similar to the "pssst" we use. It is a clandestine call, something not for everyone.

This word is used, in this sense, to describe God calling to insects: "It shall come to pass in that day that the Lord will whistle for the fly that is in the farthest part of the rivers of Egypt, and for the bee that is in the land of Assyria" (Isa. 7:18).

There are a couple of observations tied to this idea of God's small whisper that are simply too good to pass up. First, there is the idea of the *reach* of God. One only needs to glance at a map to see the far reach of God's smallest whisper in the passage before us. He calls to tiny—imperceptible to the human eye unless magnified—brains of the insects flung as far south as the Nile and as far north as the upper regions of the Euphrates. With their limited intellectual capacity and great distances to travel, He need only hiss and they come without exception.

Second, we cannot afford to miss the *rustle* of His call. This call is not a shout, not a roaring wind we Pentecostals love. It is a simple whisper, the rustle across the leaves brought by a gentle breeze. It is similar to the "still small voice" which came to the prophet Elijah when God simply was not present in the fire, raging windstorm, or the earthquake (1 Kings 19). God is calling. The question remains whether or not we will silence ourselves to hear *His* voice.

In a time when so many are writing off the church, relegating any who call for something supernatural to the background, it is a great source of comfort to know He need only hiss and those who desire His power and passion will experience a glorious renewal. And, in spite of how far you have fallen, how distant you think you are from where you need to be, all it will take is a simple "yes" to His call and He will surge into your life with speed and dispatch that will amaze all who care to notice.

This demands responsiveness on our part. If we are going to receive MORE from God, we have to be ready to act without having to be pummeled into action. While I am grateful that our Father is willing to squeeze us until we cry out for conformity to His will, I am anxious to come to the place where He need only whisper, make a simple gesture, and like the insect kingdom, I am ready to answer His call.

What would happen if we came together to worship and were ready to immediately respond to the slightest nudge from the Holy Spirit? Imagine worship where we did not have to be cajoled, "warmed up," dragged in, awakened—whatever terms you choose to describe the vast majority of time we call worship. It would be amazing to enter a time of worship and, from the outset, people worshiped! No begging, no one stiff because they did not get their way—just people responding to God's call, "*Worship Me.*"

To take things a step further, imagine what would happen in America if the millions of us who claim to be Spirit-filled started living so responsive to God's voice that we stopped to pray when He nudged us. What would take place in this nation if millions of people started living so responsive to Him that we pulled over and wept over lost cities . . . actually stopped our busy lives and told that person He burdened us for that He loved them . . . actually got up from our comfortable homes and were led to go pray for the sick? Here is what would happen—*revolution!*

Restoration

The surest marker of God's presence is when restoration takes place. God is interested in far more than emotional manipulation. He comes to set people free. He comes to restore that which has been destroyed. If there is one thing we can all rejoice over, it is the fact that God promises when He shows up, we do not have to remain the way we are!

God is really "into" this business of *restoration*:

- "Indeed He says, 'It is too small a thing that You should be My Servant to raise up the tribes of Jacob, and to *restore* the preserved ones of Israel; I will also give You as a light to the Gentiles, that You should be My salvation to the ends of the earth'" (Isa. 49:6).
- "I have seen his ways, and will heal him; I will also lead him, and *restore* comforts to him and to his mourners" (57:18).
- "'They shall be carried to Babylon, and there they shall be until the day that I visit them,' says the Lord. 'Then I will bring them up and *restore* them to this place'" (Jer. 27:22).
- "'I will *restore* health to you and heal you of your wounds,' says the Lord, 'because they called you an outcast saying: "This is Zion; no one seeks her"'" (30:17).
- "I will *restore* to you the years that the swarming locust has eaten, the crawling locust, the consuming locust, and the chewing locust, My great army which I sent among you" (Joel 2:25).
- "The Lord will *restore* the excellence of Jacob like the excellence of Israel, for the emptiers have emptied them out and ruined their vine branches" (Nah. 2:2).
- "Then I will *restore* to the peoples a pure language, that they all may call on the name of the Lord, to serve Him with one accord" (Zeph. 3:9).

God is a God of restoration! Unlike so many of us—who love to stand around and speculate when someone stumbles, and who are prone to shout out messages of condemnation when someone hits a hard spot—God instead says He is going to wade out into the brokenness of their lives and bring them back again!

I am glad my God is not the modern church. The key spiritual "gift" of many in today's church is that of condemnation. If someone falters, many are so fast to respond with assurances they knew it was coming, that the person who is down is only reaping what they deserve.

Many years ago when, while serving in the capacity as senior adult minister at a local church, I led a rather large group on a Christmas outing. We had a blast! We ate like there was no tomorrow and enjoyed ourselves like every day was Christmas. Then, on a spur-of-the-moment decision, we took a detour through an inner-city area where the lights of Christmas were prominent. Driving slowly down a main avenue, with the Christmas twinkles dancing off our eyes, we came to an intersection and our vision shifted. Loitering around that particular intersection was a gathering of some "ladies of the evening." Eyeing the pitiful sight of women reduced to selling their bodies for existence, one of the members of my group—and I remind you these were "Spirit-filled saints"—remarked out loud, "They ought to be burned, every one of 'em!"

I tried to issue a little levity by saying, "Well, Merry Christmas to you too!" But it was too late. She simply had the nerve to express what so many of that group felt. To them, those ladies didn't deserve any mercy; they deserved judgment! And, were it up to most of that group, judgment is exactly what they would get.

The problem I see with their attitude is that it is polemically opposite that of the God who redeemed us. Rather than sitting in the secluded safety of a church bus and issuing fiery condemnations, He has decided He will invade the wretched brokenness of our lives and restore us. Think of it . . . God has said He intends to come out where we are and bring us back to Him! Frankly, I can't think of any better news today. He wants to come to where we are so we can have MORE of Him!

No, It Doesn't Matter How Far Away You Are!

So many in the church today struggle because we seem to be so far from where God would have us be. It's like we have lost our moorings and we are adrift. The simple truth is, no matter how far from God's desirable place we may be at this moment, we are not too far for Him to reach into our lives and bring us back.

Notice what the Lord said through Zechariah: "I will sow them among the peoples, and they shall remember Me in far countries; they shall live, together with their children, and they shall return" (10:9).

God's people had been placed in distant, remote places—places far from what they were accustomed to. Due to a geographical dispersion—and don't forget, God was squarely involved in their scattering—they had been placed in some tenuous positions.

We know from their writings that they experienced many of the same feelings and problems we encounter today. It was hard for them to keep going. It was a drain on them to maintain their belief in God when they were living in a land with ungodly customs. They struggled to maintain a positive outlook when they realized how much they had lost and how far they had fallen. Listen to some of their own writings from this era of their history: "By the rivers of Babylon, there we sat down, yea, we wept when we remembered Zion. We hung our harps upon the willows in the midst of it. For there those who carried us away captive asked of us a song, and those who plundered us requested mirth, saying, 'Sing us one of the songs of Zion!' How shall we sing the Lord's song in a foreign land?" (Ps. 137:1-4).

It is easy to become discouraged when you are struggling to live for God and no one else seems to be your companion. It is easy to become disappointed when the culture in which you live seems to be on an ever-increasing slide downward toward the pit of hell. Many of us in America seem to have adopted the attitude of ancient Israel. We are encircled by an ever-increasing horde of godlessness.

With every Supreme Court season, with every political election cycle, the church in America seems to be shoved further down. Abortion, gay marriages, separation of church and state—to name just a few issues—are all going the opposite way of biblical mandates, and it seems we are powerless to stem the rising tide. On top of all that, the church as a whole seems to be running as fast as possible away from any idea of a supernatural God. Today's church has become, for the most part, a show of what man can produce when he sets his mind to be entertaining.

If you want to see a move of God, or if you are hungry for MORE than we currently have, you are shoved into the margins and labeled a fanatic. It seems easier to just hunker down and wait it out than to fight against the tide. Why struggle with trying to have God show up when it is easier to just hang your worship harp on a willow and hope Jesus comes before it gets any worse?

Here's why: *God knew where we were headed long before we started this journey, and He's prepared a way out if we are willing to accept it!* God knew we would be in the morass we find ourselves in today long before any of us started our journey. He knew you would be in the financial situation you are in. He knew about the struggle with a besetting sin you fight. He knew about the devastating loss you have endured. He knew all about the isolation you feel. He knew about everything long in advance, and He has made a way out for all of us!

Here's the really good news: When a man or woman—or a church or a nation for that matter—decides to move closer to God, to open their situation up to His involvement, there are no obstacles that can withstand their approach! God will see to it that people who seek for Him find exactly what they look for.

Pastors such as me have for years lamented the "balcony"—a necessary evil in churches, or at least we once thought they were, before newer designs came along. Balconies presented something akin to the "great gulf" affixed between Abraham's bosom and Lazarus in the torments of hell. For years we struggled with "losing people between the balcony and the altar." It seemed people would start toward an altar to meet with God and then get sidetracked in a foyer once they exited the balcony. In reality, when a person decides they are coming to God, it will take a lot more than a foyer where a balcony empties to keep them away! Simply put, if we want MORE of Him, nothing is going to be able to stop us.

Consider the hindrances you face in light of this proclamation of God: "He shall pass through the sea with affliction, and strike the waves of the sea: all the depths of the River shall dry up. Then the pride of Assyria shall be brought down, and the scepter of Egypt shall depart" (Zech. 10:11).

God made it clear: He was going to restore them, and nothing was going to withstand their advance. No force, regardless of its strength, can stand in the way of a man or woman—or a church for that matter—making the decision to passionately pursue the Almighty.

Obstacles can't hinder you. Those things standing in our way—things as big as the sea and as broad and powerful as a river—are really powerless to stop us. Those uncrossable things you gaze on cannot keep you from His presence. Those giant things, magnified a thousand times by our accuser, fall like dry twigs in a tornadic wind when we decide to go after MORE of God. All the tactics of the Enemy—the myriad of insults he hurls and devices he uses—fall flat before the One who calls us to His side. Debts, sicknesses, besetting sins, critical spirits, the past—*all those terrible things that have heretofore hindered us from obtaining MORE of His glory will melt like wax in a fire when we respond to His call!*

Sure, we face some tough challenges. Some of us have a long way to go in the area of being released from the past and overcoming some deep wounds. I would never seek to belittle another person's struggle, nor do I wish for mine to be made light of. Face it--we all have those "mountainous" obstacles in our lives which, if we let them, will keep us from going after MORE of His glory. It should come as no surprise that those gone before us endured the same agony.

Even Zechariah, as covered with the Spirit of God as was he, faced mountainous obstacles. Those around him who sought to bring back a move of God to the people likewise were intimidated by huge setbacks and problems. It's interesting that one of the favorite passages in the Old Testament concerning the power of the Holy Spirit comes from this very seedbed: "This is the word of the Lord to Zerubbabel: 'Not by might nor by power, but by My Spirit,' says the Lord of hosts. 'Who are you, O great mountain? Before Zerubbabel you shall become a plain! And he shall bring forth the capstone with shouts of "Grace, grace to it!"'" (Zech. 4:6-7).

All those obstacles that present themselves as immovable will fall flat at His presence. Every hindrance that seems so large to us today will appear as trivial once we have encountered MORE of His glory.

It's not that I sit and pine for something of long-gone days. It's not that I have become older and nostalgic and long for a return to a form that has worn thin. My passion has nothing to do with form, structure, or even a name. It has everything to do with the fact that I face obstacles in my life, and know so many others in the same boat, and I have learned it will take more than a good message, a sharp presentation, and a cool fellowship group to deal with those mountains.

How interesting it is to take a close look at what Zechariah said would be shouted, not once, but twice, at the obstacle—"Grace, grace." Two times (obviously for emphasis) we are told that Zerubbabel would bring forth the capstone and lay it on the crushed rubble of the mountainous obstacle that was fallen. He would not come—as some would have us believe—screaming curses at the devil or declaring some magical mantra that would produce a mystical victory. Instead, two times he was to shout "grace!" The word grace comes from a primitive Hebrew root word that indicates the leaning over of a superior to an inferior. It also was used to describe the slanted rays of the sun in the late evening, as they bent their way earthward. It's an obvious description of the fact the mountains were piles of rubble because a Greater had come to the aid of a lesser. We must remember, it's not our ingenuity and creativeness that breaks the yoke; it is the anointing of the Spirit! Be as creative as possible, but never become so immersed in your own abilities that you actually think the obstacles are moved because of you. It's Him . . . His presence!

I long for Him to come in much the same fashion as Isaiah, and for the same reason: "Oh, that You would rend the heavens! That You would come down! That the mountains might shake at Your presence" (Isa. 64:1).

The church I see needs more than a great worship team can provide. The church in America needs far more than eloquent preachers can speak into existence. Our nation deserves better than the slick programs we have. Simply put, our best efforts might attract a crowd searching for the desired religious services, but the mountains we face are not being moved by eloquence and organizational efforts. We need MORE of Him to come and shake those things to their very foundations that we, like Joshua and his followers, might walk upon our mountains once they have crumbled before us.

Obstinacy won't be able to stop you! If there is a word that describes the efforts of our Enemy, it has to be *obstinate*. He is prideful, overbearing, and obnoxious. He never quits! But that can't stop us from obtaining MORE of God! "He shall pass through the sea with affliction, and strike the waves of the sea: all the depths of the River shall dry up. Then the pride of Assyria shall be brought down, and the scepter of Egypt shall depart" (Zech. 10:11).

While the Enemy of all that is godly struts over us, declaring his worth and our worthlessness, our God says all that is just hot air. Sure, our Enemy is haughty, arrogant, and prideful—all hallmarks of his presence—but the lording over and mistreatment he sends the way of God's children cannot prevent us from receiving MORE of our Father's glory and love!

Satan is full of himself these days. It seems he has a solid grip on the church in America that will result in her utter degradation. He has polluted us with false doctrine, lulled us with prosperity, deceived us with the allure of numbers, and sidetracked us from our mission by getting our focus off a move of God's Spirit. But his days are numbered! And I don't mean by the coming of the Lord. He is on the edge of an all-out assault of those who refuse to listen any longer to his blustery threats and condescending comments by those who "know better." Make no mistake about it—there will be those, even in increasingly pagan America, who long for MORE. Those who dare to endure the attacks of a godless culture that really wants us all to go away will experience a fresh outpouring that will change us from pitiful sheep to powerful steeds of battle.

We Have Never Been Here Before!

As a matter of fact, so great will be the transformation God brings, His people will go to heights never before achieved. That's right; we still have greater days ahead! "I will also bring them back from the land of Egypt, and gather them from Assyria. I will bring them into the land of Gilead and Lebanon, until no more room is found for them" (Zech. 10:10).

God told them they were going to inhabit places in Gilead and Lebanon, places they had never inhabited before. Those were heights they had never conquered—areas they had never ruled.

God wasn't just going to bring them back, He was going to flow so mightily through them that they were going to be more powerful than ever before!

Our Father isn't interested in just making us feel better. He isn't even concerned with us "getting back to Him," whatever that may mean to you. He wants us to have MORE of Him so we can conquer those places we never overcame. Those habits you fought, but gave up on, He wants you to be free of. Those loved ones whom you have prayed for but who have never appeared interested in God, He wants so much MORE of His presence around them that they are drawn to Him. Those areas of our cities that are so dominated by spiritual darkness people are afraid to go there at night, God wants to illuminate them with spiritual freedom. That church you attend that has been dead for years, barely getting by, God wants to transform it into a powerhouse where literally hundreds of people are set free and discipled! He wants us to press forward, not sit and wait on Him to come and rescue us from a bad, old world!

"Not possible," you say? It is! It's just going to take MORE of Him being made manifest than we currently experience. Remember two things Jesus said before you surrender and decide to ride the train of just-get-by the rest of the way to heaven.

First, everything hell has cannot stop us! "I also say to you that you are Peter, and on this rock I will build My church, and the gates of Hades shall not prevail against it" (Matt. 16:18).

Obstacles and obstinacy cannot hinder us if we will walk in the power of His Spirit. With MORE of Him, there will be LESS of that!

Second, always remember that our victory is dependent on what He does in our lives. The MORE we can have Him do, the greater our victory will be. Simon Peter found that out very clearly: "And the Lord said, 'Simon, Simon! Indeed, Satan has asked for you, that he may sift you as wheat. But I have prayed for you, that your faith should not fail; and when you have returned to Me, strengthen your brethren'" (Luke 22:31-32).

He is praying for us! Let's open our hearts for MORE of what He wants to give.

Chapter 6

WHEN THINGS ARE REALLY BAD!

> They shall be like mighty men, who tread down their enemies in the mire of the streets in the battle. They shall fight because the Lord is with them, and the riders on horses shall be put to shame (Zech. 10:5).

One of the things we have done—in fact, many Christians through the centuries have led the way in this—is to ignore the Lord until things grew so bad we were backed into a corner and reached a place of such desperation, and then we cried out to God with ardor and abandon. Our God, being ever merciful and gracious, has heard our plea and come to our rescue more than once. History is stacked with examples of seasons where His people were in dire straits, mainly from their own doings, and when they cried out with passionate repentance, He came rushing to their aid.

The climate in which we currently reside, spiritually speaking, has caused many to decry the future of the church. Read any study done by brutally honest research groups, and they all pretty much point to the same finding: the church in America is in deep trouble. If we shave away the Pollyanna platitudes and get down to the real truth of the matter, we can see their dire predictions have a great amount of truth to them. Such reality has caused some alarming statements to be uttered over the last few years. For instance, Randy Bright, writing in the *Tulsa Beacon*, stated, "The future of the American church looks a bit bleak." An opinion based on research (*The AmericanChurch.org*) reveals the prognostication that forty-nine of fifty states will see a decrease in church attendance over the next forty years. Even in the South, where the buckle of the Bible Belt is still firmly latched, there is an expectation of a more than 20 percent decline in church attendance during this same time period!

Barna, the guru of research entities among the faithful, released a sobering set of facts a few years ago. When polled about the issues that mattered most to them, respondents placed "advancing the health of America's churches" dead last in their concerns. It doesn't help at all that a Pew Forum survey recently revealed we, particularly the Evangelicals, are now known more for our political views than our religious beliefs. It appears we have once more backed ourselves into a corner, and it is again time for us to cease our hand-wringing over what we are going to do with this gone-mad culture and instead apply the age-old remedy proposed by our God. We need to fall on our faces and cry aloud for revival and restoration—for MORE!

Stuck!

Zechariah used a word in verse 5 that resonates with our situation today—he spoke of "mire." This Hebrew term speaks of mud, or clay. It is also a vivid picture of being stuck (or trapped) in the circumstance around you. This is the word used to describe the imprisoning muck into which Jeremiah sank when he was so roughly treated by Zedekiah: "So they took Jeremiah and cast him into the dungeon of Malchiah the king's son, which was in the court of the prison, and they let Jeremiah down with ropes. And in the dungeon there was no water, but mire. So Jeremiah sank in the mire" (Jer. 38:6).

If you have ever ventured into a swamp and tried to walk around, you know firsthand the experience Jeremiah endured. Being stuck in the mire is a draining, exhausting, nasty affair. It can leave you weary, battered, and thankful to be alive.

This lets you in on part of my youth that offers nothing but a glimpse into a simpler time, but I had an encounter with being stuck in the mire that qualifies me to elaborate a bit. When two friends of mine and I were in our early teens, we would invade the swamps caused by beavers, tear out the beaver dams, and later in the evening, go back in and shoot snakes. Truth be told, we murdered them by the bushels! In fact, had the three of us not inflicted such carnage on those reptiles with our trusty .22 rifles, the world would probably be overcome with snakes today!

One particularly muggy spring afternoon, my two friends and I ventured deep into the bog in search of new territory. Little did we know a powerful thunderstorm that would produce a large tornado was headed our way. I can remember it as if it were yesterday. One moment we are slogging through the mud, my rubber hip boots keeping me safe and dry, and the next moment we were caught in a maelstrom of howling winds, snapping trees, and an adrenaline rush unlike any I have ever experienced.

There was, however, one major problem: Anytime I took a step, like Jeremiah, I would sink about two feet into the mire. Trust me, when a tornado is bearing down on you and trees are literally flying through the air around you, the last feeling you wish to experience is being stuck in the mire! You can't move . . . you can't shuffle—you are stuck and at the mercy of your surroundings. To make matters worse, all I could see of my buddies was the churning of their arms and legs as they, not wearing same equipment as I was, were headed for higher ground and safety.

Perhaps you, like me, periodically endure moments similar to my experience that day in that storm-strewn swamp. While my buddies were headed for brighter days, I was stuck like a fly on flypaper in my muddy hole. They were going to make it; I was destined to die in a swamp. The analogies are obvious and simple. How many times have I read about the exploits of my fellows, while I seemed doomed to serve in the hidden muddy holes of the world? How many times have I read about the great accomplishments of others while I seemed relegated to the backwaters, so to speak, of the Kingdom? How many times have you gone to some type of large meeting and listened to the latest "Wonder Boy" in the harvest regale in his lofty proficiencies, while you sat there and wondered if you were forever destined to remain in your stormy swamp?

The harsh truth is, being stuck in the mire is no fun. What's more, if you stay there, you will die in your muddy hole. Obviously, I made it out that day, or else I wouldn't be recalling that whole affair. While the storms were swirling around me, I decided I didn't want to die there, so I acted. I started churning my legs until my lungs burned. In fact, I shed those large rubber boots and ran out with bare feet. I never did find those boots! I charged out of that death trap with as much energy and determination as any soldier on D-Day used hitting a beach in Normandy. When I came to a barbed wire fence in my way, I hit the ground at full tilt, slid under that obstacle with as much grim determination as any Ranger trainee sliding under wire with live fire going off over his head. I meant to get out of there, regardless!

Did it cost me? Yes! I sunk my only .22 rifle into the mud when I fell, and it never worked the same again. I lost my prized possession—my rubber boots. My feet were laced with cuts, and I had scrapes and bruises from flying debris. But I made it out.

Here's what we need to remember when things are really bad—*there is a way out of the mire!* I got out of mine. Jeremiah got out of his. And the word of the Lord to us today is, *When MORE comes, the very mire in which we are trapped will be used by the Holy Spirit to enable us to conquer!* It may be bad, really bad, where you are right now. Life and the overwhelming circumstances you face may in fact be so preponderant, you cannot see a way out. Don't give up and surrender to the negative press around you. Hide yourself away and cry out until MORE of His glory shows up, and then go forth and defeat your enemies right where you now feel so entrapped.

Can It Happen Here . . . to Me?

To understand just how powerful our God is, we need to take a trip with another Old Testament prophet, Ezekiel. He found himself facing a rather nasty situation one day. Although this passage has been preached a million times, let's see if one more visit can produce hope for us today. After all, if God can show up with MORE for him in the dilemma in which he found himself, surely He can visit us again and bring a return of His glory to our lives.

Desolation

"The hand of the Lord came upon me and brought me out in the Spirit of the Lord, and set me down in the midst of the valley; and it was full of bones. Then He caused me to pass by them all around, and behold, there were very many in the open valley; and indeed they were very dry. And He said to me, 'Son of man, can these bones live?' So I answered, 'O Lord God, You know'" (Ezek. 37:1-3).

How many pastors have gone through this experience? Looking out on a Sunday, all one can see is a dried-out, what-used-to-be place. Taking a look from another angle, how many believers today are living Ezekiel's experiences? Looking at their life, all they see is missed opportunities, wasted resources, and bad decisions. The situation of this prophet is one we all can identify with on some level. I call it a "desolate place."

Desolate places are littered with what used to be. Scattered all around are reminders that something had at one time been filled with promise, ripe with potential, but now is nothing but an empty shell that rattles like dried-up bones in a shaking wind. Think about what greeted Ezekiel's gaze that day. At one time, there had been a powerful army. They had marched with determination and gusto, eager to go forth into battle for their king. Their footsteps had caused the enemy to quiver in fear, hide in the caves, and run for their very lives. They had been such a strong, unbending force.

However, somewhere along the way, something had happened. Something, or some things, had led to their decline and ultimate destruction. For some reason, a once mighty force had been reduced to mere rubble. What could possibly have led to such demise?

Could it have been a series of bad choices? Could they, like the wending sheep of Zechariah's day, have listened to the wrong voices and made some terrible decisions? Perhaps there had arisen in the camp insistent voices that caught the ear of leadership, which were determined to take care of their own interests rather than that of the entire army. It is possible that a few charismatic leaders arose who were so set on building their reputation and their small segment of the army that they ignored, to the utter detriment of the whole, that which had brought success thus far. It is possible that senior leadership, in an attempt to stave off a perceived threat of a coup, gave in to these pressing voices in order to keep the peace and hold the army together.

Maybe it wasn't a series of bad choices; perhaps they lost sight of their reason for existence. It could very well be that over time, due to hardships endured and the human nature being what it is, they grew weary of all the marching, drilling, fighting, deprivation—all the stuff associated with warfare—and decided they were just going to sit down and settle right where they were. They could have simply lost sight of the fact they were not their own—they were the possession of a king who had sent them into battle for a cause—and rest wasn't going to be a reality for them until all wars had ceased and they were finally in the immediate presence of their king.

Who knows, they might have even decided to shift tactics and make buddies with the enemy. Instead of standing toe-to-toe in battle, they might have hit upon the idea of getting along, not making waves, and doing whatever it took to woo the enemy into the camp so they could then win them over with their winsome smiles and slick entertainment. Then, the "aha" moment came when it finally dawned on them they had made a tragic mistake and now the enemy was greater than they and the outcome was inevitable. They were going down!

History is silent about this one. All we know is, what once was great now was relegated to the dustbin of time. Where there had been a mighty force for the king now lay scattered remnants of power. What once was filled with promise and potential, now was devastated, blighted, and shoved to the periphery. It was desolation.

Before You Stop Reading!

Before you throw this book down and give up because you feel so bad, keep reading! When MORE comes your way, things change! Far too many of us are stuck at this juncture. In fact, far too many of us have decided to sit on the hillside of the bone yard and lament our situation, while God is over in the corner of our lives waiting on us to become engaged with Him.

At times I have sat at the gateway of such cemeteries and lamented my plight, so I know the typical reactions we entertain. We love to *blame* our predecessors who allowed the paucity of results to take place. It is their fault, not ours; they did it, not me. Ezekiel had nothing to do with the desolation set before him. He had not made one bad choice, allowed one dissenting voice, nor encouraged one forgetful moment. If anyone could have played the blame game, he could have.

It is interesting that in the entire engagement between Ezekiel and God, there was never even a chance given for "who did what." The blame game does nothing but drain us of energy for what lies ahead and reveals our utter lack of knowledge about what matters to God. Do you remember the incident where Jesus healed a man of blindness "and His disciples asked Him, saying, 'Rabbi, who sinned, this man or his parents, that he was born blind?'" (John 9:2).

Slice that one any way you want to, spin it with any background information you like—that was a stupid question! But it goes to the heart of our human, carnal nature. We love to lay blame. It is that compulsion that has driven a deep tent peg into the ground and has kept so many of us sitting and staring at dry bones. We want to know who is to blame for this, while God is more interested in moving forward and giving us MORE of His glory so things can change!

Some of us have moved beyond the *blame* game. We know we have made enough mistakes of our own that there are going to be some headhunters looking for us down the road as they stare at the remains of our mistakes. No, we don't blame, but we love to *bemoan* our situation. Who's to blame is not our passion; "woe is me" is the grand marshal of our parade.

Ezekiel could have easily fallen prey to this hallmark of reasons why we aren't accomplishing anything. After all, as far as we can tell, he didn't even ask for his assignment. He simply recalls his adventure by telling us this: "The hand of the Lord came upon me and brought me . . . down in the midst of the valley" (Ezek. 37:1).

The first time this idea of the hand of God coming *upon* something is very early in the Bible. It is a powerful picture: "And the earth was without form, and void; and darkness was upon the face of the deep. And the Spirit of God moved upon the face of the waters" (Gen. 1:2 KJV).

Both times the word *upon* is used in the Creation narrative, it is the same term used to describe the compulsion of Ezekiel into his desolate place. Ezekiel didn't ask for that spot—God shoved him, moved him, molded him, acted upon him until he arrived at a dried-up bone yard of what used to be! If anyone deserved to employ the bemoaning syndrome, Ezekiel could have moved to the head of the class. If anyone had the right to employ the term "burned-over field" or "hopeless situation," Ezekiel earned such a claim.

However, there is not a shred of conversation between the man and his God about how unfair his situation was. Having been a whiner to God (and sometimes to man) about how unjust my plight was at the moment, I am ashamed when I encounter this text. God wasn't interested in Ezekiel's self-pity. The desolate "had been's" were not interested either. Cell phones and Twitter accounts didn't exist during his time, so he couldn't even contact his buddies, most of whom didn't care either; they just listened out of friendship. Nothing was out there but a man who didn't deserve his situation and a God who was going to use him to bring MORE of His presence into a desolate spot.

If you, like Ezekiel, today find yourself staring at desolation, this might be a good time to slow down and ponder a couple of important facts relating to the less-than-perfect situation in which you find yourself.

First of all, God knew right where the bones were. He took Ezekiel there as if He had been there before. No one stopped for a map to the dry-bones graveyard. No one dug out the GPS tracking device to type in a search function. The God who carried Ezekiel to that desolate place knew precisely where they were headed. God had already been there, mapped things out, and was keenly aware of what was needed. Despite the fact bad choices had been made, God still kept up with them. Regardless of the misguiding voices that had arisen in their midst and which had contributed to their demise, God still had them on His radar.

Quite frankly, I draw great comfort from the idea that He knows where I am. Even though I may be in the most desolate, barren place of my life, God knows exactly where I am. I may even be here because I made some really bad decisions in the past, but He hasn't written me off. In fact, I may be so far removed from the hustle and bustle of the movers and shakers in the world I am like a forgotten pile of dead men's bones, but He knows where I am.

Have you ever considered how desolate things must have looked to Noah? Alone, afloat, with nothing but smelly animals and an overworked family crew, Noah had to wonder at times if God had placed him where he was, but then forgotten his plight. I love the way Moses, through the unction of the Holy Spirit, penned the following: "Then God remembered Noah, and every living thing, and all the animals that were with him in the ark. And God made a wind to pass over the earth, and the waters subsided" (Gen. 8:1).

It wasn't that God had forgotten about Noah. God doesn't forget in that sense. This word "remembered" means God recalled His promise and acted in accordance with His covenant. While things looked bleak from the perspective of those on board that floating lifeline, nothing at all changed from God's vantage point. He was in complete control regardless of how desolate things looked to the participants.

This is a difficult lesson to learn—at least it has been, and continues to be, for me—but God knows exactly where the desolate place resides. He hasn't forgotten it, written it off, or put it down as a loss on the bottom line. In fact, He has—to borrow some lines from an old song—"walked the dark hills so He can guide you and me."

Equally important is this fact: God wasn't through with that desolate situation. He still had a plan for their future. While everyone else had passed by, cleaned up the funeral flowers, and written some nice eulogies, God was busy setting His plan for MORE of His glory in motion. If the Bible teaches us anything, it teaches us to look beyond the proclamations of man that a situation is lost and to see God at work behind the scenes.

A favorite passage of many people is buried within the painful words of Jeremiah: "For I know the thoughts that I think toward you, says the Lord, thoughts of peace and not of evil, to give you a future and a hope" (29:11).

It has been my discovery that very few people who cite that verse as a favorite have any understanding of the context. God didn't utter those comforting words to a group of graduating seminary students who had just gone through a six-week, campus-shaking, city-awakening revival. Instead, it was penned to a group of captives who had made such glaringly bad decisions that God had slapped them with invasion and deportation. Yet even those calamitous events had not demurred God from His commitment to their advancement.

Fast-forward several hundred years and walk with crestfallen disciples as they move, from a safe distance of course, with a burial cortege, taking the mutilated body of Jesus to a borrowed grave. If dictionaries came with pictures to describe words, *desolation* might well have that portrait as the epitome of meaning. Unbeknownst to all gathered around that somber scene, God was working mightily through that lifeless body to snap the back of the Serpent and bring everlasting life to all mankind. Just because things were bad at the moment did not mean they would stay that way. Nor does the stubborn refusal of our situation today to accept a mighty move of God mean it will always play the trump card. Our God has this amazing proclivity to show up in the most desolate of places with MORE of His glory, resulting in the most stunning of visitations of His Spirit.

Diminished Vision

Ezekiel wasn't simply struggling with the desolation around him. He had fallen prey to an arch nemesis that decimates so many of us today. Ezekiel was suffering from a horrible case of diminished vision. Listen closely and you can hear it in his voice, his response to a question posed by God. "And He said to me, 'Son of man, can these bones live?' So I answered, 'O Lord God, You know'" (Ezek. 37:3).

Consider for a moment his situation. Ezekiel was not a novice when it came to the matters of supernatural power. He was well versed in the matters pertaining to the greatness of God.

For instance, when he was growing up, he lived under the influence of Jeremiah. Serving in priestly family and as a priest himself, he knew firsthand the stories of God's power in the past. It is likely Ezekiel and Daniel knew each other prior to the age of captivity, so it can easily be inferred he was keenly aware of the exploits of his compatriot and the mighty display of God's glory in his life.

One only need examine the opening visions he recounts in his writings to see Ezekiel was very familiar with the power of the Almighty: "Now it came to pass in the thirtieth year, in the fourth month, on the fifth day of the month, as I was among the captives by the River Chebar, that the heavens were opened and I saw visions of God" (1:1).

He saw things we are grappling with today. Images of the glory and power of God flooded his heart, soul, his very being, until he was so immersed in the snippets of God's glory that he was powerless to do anything but remain there until the Master had laid out what He wanted the man to see. It started with a raging storm, hurtling itself from the north onto the house of Israel. Swirling winds, powerful claps of thunder, and raging chaos ruled the scene. Images of creatures that still mystify, coupled with difficult-to-grasp ideas of wheels and fire burst into view. It must have been terribly disconcerting to this priest now called to be a prophet.

There is something you and I need to cling to, however, hardly noticeable unless one pays close attention. Toward the end of this opening salvo of God's glory, Ezekiel gives us a word of comfort when we are facing really difficult times: "Like the appearance of a rainbow in a cloud on a rainy day, so was the appearance of the brightness all around it. This was the appearance of the likeness of the glory of the Lord" (1:28).

Ezekiel saw a rainbow. The glory of the Lord radiated like a rainbow. Remember, Noah saw a rainbow after the storm was over (Gen. 9). We love those, don't we? That ribbon of color in the sky indicates the worst is past. John the Revelator saw a rainbow just before the greatest storm this world will ever witness begins (Rev. 4). I find it a mighty comfort to know heaven didn't change much (except for the inhabitants, of course) between the time it opened and Ezekiel saw it by a river in Babylon, and hundreds of years later when John was called up and saw it with a pure crystal river flowing through it. But most of all, perhaps greater to me at this season of life, is the fact Ezekiel saw the rainbow not before or after the storm, but rather residing above it. Yes, a storm was headed his way that would rock his world. We believers, particularly American believers, need to let this sink in. A storm was coming which would shake the very foundations of his world, *but God was still residing over it all, in complete control!*

I refuse to acquiesce to the modern "isms" which seem to be springing up like pesky weeds in a garden, seeking to dilute our Father's status and power. I denounce the very idea our God is not in complete and utter control of the events swirling around us. I denounce with vehemence the theology being embraced by many who espouse the notion our God doesn't know what lies ahead, that every day and decision made by man presents Him with a new set of problems. I decry the very idea that our God is engaged in a cosmic struggle with evil, and still ponders the idea He might not win. The modernist approach, which relegates God to the corners of our churches and the peripheries of our mission, should be neatly packaged and thrown out with the trash. Our God is the same God in control when Ezekiel caught this small glimpse into heaven. He hasn't changed, and He can't change. He is still the same today as He was that day—in control, over it all, in charge, and working His will.

Sounds Good, but I Just Don't Know!

My problem, perhaps yours as well, tends to be the same conundrum faced by Ezekiel. It goes like this: *When all you can see is desolation, you tend to suffer from diminished vision.*

Back to the question God posed: "Can these bones come back to life?" You would think the immediate answer from a man who had seen all Ezekiel had seen and been through all that man had been through was, "You'd better believe it!" After all, isn't that what we expect, even demand? Yet here is this man of God . . . a man who wrote one of the longest books in the Bible . . . a book filled, incidentally, with dreams and visions that still baffle scholars to this day . . . and his meek, demurring answer to the thunderous God is, "I don't know . . . only You know the answer to that one."

"I don't read that in the text," you say. You are right. Perhaps I am taking too much literary license, but I don't think so. I think Ezekiel, in spite of the fact he had been through mighty moves of God, was so intently staring at the desolation around him that the miry situation in which he found himself left him struggling with diminished vision. Like so many of us today, when asked about whether or not God can do great things in our lives and our churches, we give the well-worn religious bromide, "I know God can!" Unstated, because it sounds so unreligious, is the second part, "I just don't know if He will."

In all fairness, I have no stones to throw at the prophet. Equally important, I have no stones to throw at anyone else who is stuck in the mire of a desolate situation and struggles to keep the faith that God will help them. It's simply too easy to get our focus off God and on the grave situation around us. (I ought to know . . . I have Ph.D. in "grave situation staring.")

No, my task is not to belittle anyone who struggles with diminished vision. Bearing the scars on my psyche from going to far too many meetings where some "superstar" up front castigated all us "little guys" out there for not being as stellar as he, I no longer possess the energy or inclination to put anyone down. (By the way, get to know those superstars and you will discover they have their own diminished vision moments—they just won't talk about them!) My passion is to encourage you to simply look in another direction. Not at the bony desolation that seems utterly hopeless. Not even at the books and instructions of the latest "hero" who "has done it." Rather, shift your gaze just a little higher. Look just above your desolate situation, keep on scanning past the hawkers of the latest success books and tapes, and catch a fleeting glimpse of the One who called you, who saved you, who will be the One to deliver you.

Look up and see the glory of God. See the One who possesses all the power needed to bring victory into your life. See the One who can utterly change your desolate place into a paradise of victory.

If your church really grows, really starts winning hundreds of lost people, it will be His doing, not yours. If your family suddenly turns around and is saved, it will not be due to your constant barrage of how lost they are; it will be due to His invasion of their lives. Mark it down: if you are healed of some horrible disease, it will not be credited to the fact the latest man-of-the-kingdom blew into your town for a crusade. It will be due to the fact God lavished His power upon your body. Once more, we need to blend our voices with those of the psalmist's era, when he penned words sung by the boy Jesus as He trudged up the hillsides, going to Jerusalem to the feasts.

> I will lift up my eyes to the hills—From whence comes my help? My help comes from the Lord, who made heaven and earth. He will not allow your foot to be moved; He who keeps you will not slumber. Behold, He who keeps Israel shall neither slumber nor sleep. The Lord is your keeper; the Lord is your shade at your right hand. The sun shall not strike you by day, nor the moon by night. The Lord shall preserve you from all evil; He shall preserve your soul. The Lord shall preserve your going out and your coming in from this time forth, and even forevermore (Ps. 121).

Look above; get alone with Him until you see His glory again. Then, as the eyes of the servant of Elisha in 2 Kings 6 were opened, so your eyes can be opened as well to the fact that "those who are with us are more than those who are against us!" (see v. 16).

Your God is an awesome God. You don't need less of Him—you need MORE! And MORE is precisely what He is offering, if we are willing to receive.

Dependent People

If you find yourself in the mire, stuck while the world speeds by, you are going to need more than man can offer. If you are in a desolate place, staring at shattered dreams and lamenting what could have been to the point of desperation, a nice little chat from a charming and ebullient speaker might make you feel better, but it won't do much to extract you from the prison of mire that holds you tightly. You need more than man, with all his brilliance, can give; you need the Word of God.

Take a moment to examine what brought about the transformation in Ezekiel's sorry situation. "Again He said to me, 'Prophesy to these bones, and say to them, "O dry bones, hear the word of the Lord!"'" (Ezek. 37:4).

It was the word of the Lord that made the difference, not Ezekiel's word. It wasn't some big-time prophet's word. We just saw how fallible prophets are. He wasn't even sure it would work. But he spoke the word of the Lord. As a matter of fact, beginning with verse 5, we read three times, "Thus says the Lord God" (vv. 5, 9, 12).

When you are stuck in the mire, wearied from trying to extract yourself, panicked because others are speeding by, frustrated because every move you make seems to be a setback, don't surrender to the natural inclination to quit. Begin to immerse yourself in His Word. When every program has failed; when you have bought into and tried all the late-night TV preacher schemes; when you have exhausted yourself running from one man to another, hoping this time the magic bullet will be found in a prayer line, only to remain fixed in the mire, immobile and going nowhere, don't throw in the towel, concluding nothing works. Begin to lift your eyes up and fill your mouth with God's Word. In the end, it will be His Word that triumphs.

If we are to see MORE, it is an imperative that we once again make His Word the basis of all we do. Remember, the Word of God creates special avenues for His glory. Consider the following, which are just a few of the examples of MORE that is available to us:

- Healing (Ps. 107:20)
- Deliverance from the fear of man (56:4)
- Mercy and abundant redemption (130:5-7)
- Peace like a river (Isa. 66:5-12)
- Inner fire (Jer. 20:9)

If you take the time to digest Psalm 119, you discover the ample abundance of His glorious gifts made accessible by His Word:
- Cleansing (v. 9)
- Revival (v. 25)
- Strength (v. 28)
- A security in heaven (v. 89)
- Hiding place, a shield (v. 114)

In fact, so important to the first-century church was the Word of God, when they had endured hardship and faced severe discipline from legal authorities, their prayer was for inner strength to keep on preaching His Word: "Now, Lord, look on their threats, and grant to Your servants that with all boldness they may speak Your word, by stretching out Your hand to heal, and that signs and wonders may be done through the name of Your holy Servant Jesus" (Acts 4:29-30).

They understood the inseparable connection between His Word and His power. Make no mistake about it, if we are going to witness MORE of His glory and experience the transformation and deliverance from the mire, it will come on the heels of submission to and immersion in His Word.

Remember, our God is a jealous God and will share His glory with no man. He will not tolerate flesh dominating the space reserved for Him. He alone is the centerpiece of the arena. He made that clear to Ezekiel: "Then you shall know that I am the Lord" (37:13).

He made it equally clear to Zechariah: "My anger is kindled against the shepherds, and I will punish the goatherds. For the Lord of hosts will visit His flock, the house of Judah, and will make them as His royal horse in the battle" (10:3).

It will be His doing, not some man's. He will move as His people begin to look to Him and stand on His Word.

Are you stuck? Is the need really bad? That doesn't limit God at all. Perhaps it is time we, His people, stop listening to the cacophony of voices calling to us to follow their plan, and once more settle ourselves, even if we are in the mire, and start looking once more to heaven. He is the One who has answered before. Since He never changes, we can rest assured He will hear and answer again!

Chapter 7

HOW TO GET BACK

"I will sow them among the peoples, and they shall remember Me in far countries; they shall live, together with their children, and they shall return" (Zech. 10:9).

What a staggering statement made by the Lord: "They shall return." Not "possibly will come back," not even "I hope to someday see them come limping in." No, God was adamant. His scattered people, wending like wayward sheep, would return in the power He intended to sow into their lives. While I am fully aware of the Judaic focus of that powerful proclamation, I can't help but hear somewhere rumbling in the background, like distant echoes of thunder before the arrival of a downpour, an equally powerful promise: "It shall come to pass afterward that I will pour out My Spirit on all flesh; your sons and your daughters shall prophesy, your old men shall dream dreams, your young men shall see visions. And also on My menservants and on My maidservants I will pour out My Spirit in those days" (Joel 2:28-29).

Many years later, on the edge of a whirlwind of God's glory, the apostle Peter stood up and, under the anointing of that Spirit, made an equally bold explanation and declaration: "It shall come to pass in the last days, says God, that I will pour out of My Spirit on all flesh; your sons and your daughters shall prophesy, your young men shall see visions, your old men shall dream dreams. And on My menservants and on My maidservants I will pour out My Spirit in those days; and they shall prophesy" (Acts 2:17-18).

"They shall return" resonates with the same force as "I will pour out My Spirit." We can depend on our Father to fulfill His Word. Just as we have witnessed the outpouring of the Holy Spirit over the last century or so, we can witness a return to His powerful presence being manifested once more in our midst. He hasn't changed. His promise is still valid. The real decision maker in this equation seems to be us.

A Tough Question

In sharing the ideas behind this work with a mentor friend, he posed several questions, some of them straight to the point and thought-provoking. One question, "Is this happening already and we simply are not a part of it?" was one which made me step back and ponder the possibility we have become so calloused, so immersed in a culture that decries anything holy, we might indeed be possessed of such spiritual blindness we can't even see a work of God. Worse yet, could it be we have become so carnal we are now fighting against an outpouring of God's Spirit because it would invade our man-made spaces? I shudder to think we have allowed ourselves to slide so far from the fire of Pentecost we now are satisfied with the burned-out ashes of what once was, comforted by the fact we now have a larger crowd to be lukewarm with us!

However tough that question was, and it dug deep, the most probing question of all was simple and straightforward: *How do we get there?* The simple truth remains, any buzzard can point out a dead, stinking corpse. It doesn't take a spiritual giant to see the church in America is in trouble. Any statistician looking at the numbers before us can discern we are in trouble. What we need—what we must have—is someone who will rise from the cold ashes of a burned-out church and boldly lead the church back to the place where MORE of God shows up and actual transformation takes place.

Understand, there isn't a man or woman alive who can *make* God do anything. He dispenses His glory at His prerogative. All we can do is position ourselves before Him, declaring our need, and wait on His visitation. We can see this in the exhortation given us by James: "Is anyone among you sick? Let him call for the elders of the church, and let them pray over him, anointing him with oil in the name of the Lord. And the prayer of faith will save the sick, and the Lord will raise him up. And if he has committed sins, he will be forgiven" (James 5:14-15).

The sick are called upon to position themselves before praying elders. The elders are to position themselves before the Lord by anointing with oil and offering fervent prayer. Once everyone has done his particular part, it is then up to the Lord to do His work. The healing comes from God—not because a man made Him do it, but out of His abundant grace and provision.

It is the same with attempting to obtain MORE of the Lord. We can only position ourselves so that we can be recipients of His presence. Having done that, we wait on Him. Here's the good part: Every time in history a group of people decided they would position themselves for MORE of God, MORE came!

The pressing question before us, the one which haunts me, is not so much about whether or not God's glory is being poured out today, or even how we get back to the place where we are recipients of His power. No, I think the core question is one that each of us, each church, each pastor, must confront and be utterly truthful in answering: *Am I willing to do what I have to do to get MORE?* There it is—the painful, stark, harsh reality. Deep within, we all know God is more than willing to pour out His Spirit in our lives. The gnawing little thing in the back of our mind, the intruding truth we try to suppress, is the question about whether or not we are willing to do what it takes to position ourselves before God so He might bestow MORE upon us.

What Worked in Days Gone By

While it is true we live in an age of such rapid change one can scarcely keep up, and churches must adapt to the harvest they are sent to reap, we cannot make the terrible mistake of thinking God has changed along with our whims. Through all the variegated efforts of the American church to reach pagan America, God has remained precisely and unashamedly the same! In other words, what worked with God in the past will still work with God today. That should bring some comfort to those of us who are so desperate to reach a changing culture that we scurry like rabbits chased by hounds in an attempt to implement the latest "new thing." We can go to God, in an old-fashioned way, and meet the One who can turn our lives, and our churches, around!

Jonathan Edwards, no stranger to revival himself, listed five well-known steps to revival:

1. *Intercession.* Prayer is the first stepping-stone to any move of God. J. Edwin Orr, a leader for over sixty years, stated it simply: "Whenever God is ready to do something new with His people, He always sets them to praying."

2. *Revelation.* There is always a new manifestation of Jesus Christ. As we shall see shortly, if we hope to have MORE today, we must catch a fresh vision of the Cross and Christ crucified.

3. *Consecration.* God's people turn to Him anew, forsaking their sins (and to each other), doing His work.

4. *Revitalization.* Ministries become purified, regenerated, and more fruitful.

5. *Expansion.* There is a resulting greater impact upon an area, a spiritual awakening.

If such a move of God could take place in Edward's day, it can happen in ours as well. Edwards lived in a day when every third house was adversely affected by alcohol. Violence and sexual promiscuity were rampant. The church of his day had become morally corroded and was virtually ignored by the masses. *Sound familiar?* Yet, it was into that very quagmire God sent a reformation . . . MORE. If He did it for them, He will do it for us!

Now, let's go on to the hard stuff: How much of ourselves are we willing to sacrifice to see MORE? How much are we willing to give up? Ask yourself, "How far am I willing to go in order to witness MORE of His power?"

There is a disturbing image presented in Zechariah 12. It is one that I had rather not contemplate; it makes me uncomfortable. Yet it is such a revealing picture of a person, or a people, who are willing to be touched by the Lord, we cannot overlook it. "It shall happen in that day that I will make Jerusalem a very heavy stone for all peoples; all who would heave it away will surely be cut in pieces, though all nations of the earth are gathered against it" (v. 3).

MORE will result in some rather distressing events. One would think MORE would cause everyone to be jubilant, to celebrate. Such is hardly the case. In fact, if MORE of God does come your way, get ready for some surprising results. Not everyone is going to like it. As a matter of fact, some—possibly most—are going to want to get rid of His glory. Don't let that stop you. For just as Jerusalem is a "heavy stone" (politically speaking) today and cannot be shoved aside, so the glory of MORE of His presence will not be staunched by a vast horde of vocal critics or deserters. It is up to those of us who are tired of church-as-usual, wearied with watching as a couple of generations walk away from the church, to decide we know the answer and will not be satisfied until MORE of His glory once more saturates our lives and our churches. It is up to us to pay the price. The looming question remains, "Will the Lord find among us those willing to endure through the inevitable opposition?" The answer to that question may well determine the spiritual outcome of our entire nation. For sure, it will have a dramatic effect on hundreds of thousands, if not millions, of souls.

Will You Sign Up for This?

Imagine the shock felt by many of the recruits to our military. Raised on video games, warfare is, to them, a game played while sitting in an air-conditioned room with plenty of snacks and buddies nearby. It has to be a shock to the system when a drill sergeant starts screaming at them and, instead of a comfy room, they are met with bone-wearying calisthenics and hours of boring drills. We can imagine many of today's recruits, thinking they would be flying jets and unleashing powerful weapons at the push of a button, but instead finding themselves crawling through mud or clamoring over an obstacle course, exclaiming, "I didn't sign up for this!" We all know the truth—they did sign up for just what they are receiving. The harsh treatment of boot camp and specialized training is essential for elite combat troops.

This will come as a shock to many of us, raised in the comfy environs of an accepted Pentecostal experience, but harsh times are coming—indeed are already here in many quarters—for those who dare to claim the Pentecostal fire of our forefathers. Regrettably, it doesn't appear that it will become any easier as time rolls on.

It's time for us to prepare ourselves . . . to get ready for what's on the horizon . . . to steel ourselves for the inevitable hostilities which will come our direction as we seek to have a dramatic influx of Holy Spirit power. I think about an obscure command given by Paul: "Watch, stand fast in the faith, be brave, be strong" (1 Cor. 16:13).

The King James Version puts it, "Quit you like men" ("be brave"). It's time we *quit* not pressing forward, worrying about what might come our way if we press on. What we must do is going to take strong men, brave women, young people who stand fast, unmoved by the insults that will be hurled their way. In other words, don't get upset when it starts. Remember, you did sign up for this!

Criticism

Are you willing to endure criticism from the new, modern church because you dare to cling to an old path? Can you take it when the "neo-Christians" tear into you verbally because you have decided there is something in the old way you aren't willing to give up? If you are going to delve into the old paths of Holy Spirit anointed, powerful demonstrations of His Spirit, criticism will come your way. As a matter of fact, you will be deemed out of touch, lacking vision, missing the point, and some other things I can't print here. Prepare yourself for it, and don't allow the junk that will be hurled at you stop you from going back and reopening the deep wells of Pentecostal power.

How to Get Back

Lou Engle, in his great book *Digging the Wells of Revival*, tells the story of Isaac reopening the wells of his father (Gen. 26). The Philistines, in an effort to drive Abraham and his successors out of their promised inheritance, clogged up the wells. Naturally, in that region of the world, a working well is the most precious commodity imaginable. Since it was much easier to re-dig a well than to find the flow and dig a new source, Isaac set out to recapture the powerful essence that had sustained his father.

Isaac may have used a different bucket to draw water up. He might well have set up the appearance of the well differently than Abraham. But he knew one thing: *that stuff which came out of God's provisional hand was the very essence of his survival!* Regrettably, many of us seem to have decided if we can make a place look like a well, and come around and sing about water, it doesn't matter if there is really anything there to produce life and liberty.

Engle went on to vividly describe the criticism that is leveled at a person, or church, when they decide to return to the old ways, to seek the old power. In a conversation with a lady from the Foursquare Church, a powerful Pentecostal movement, she flatly stated, "Our church is trying to distance ourselves from that Pentecostal stuff." Imagine that—trying to distance yourself from the very power of the Holy Spirit. Think about it—trying to distance yourself from the very essence of the greatest revival and ingathering of people ever witnessed in the Kingdom.

Yet that is precisely what many "Pentecostals" are trying to do today. In our earnest efforts to silence the criticisms of those who either deny the power of the Holy Spirit or don't want His fiery presence, we have buckled to criticism and decided to court the favor of man rather than the fire of God. May He forgive us and raise up a generation of men and women who are impervious to the critical statements of unbelievers and lukewarm saints alike. May He imbue us with such rugged determination that no amount of criticism can deter us from going back to the old wells of Holy Spirit power and once more opening that flow of His glory in our lives and churches!

Critiques Over Worship

There isn't space here to really delve into the connection between an outpouring of MORE of His glory and worship. Suffice it to say, MORE isn't headed our way until we have abandoned our carnal man and entered into worship. It is here, possibly more than any other place, that we must prepare ourselves for the assaults of critical people who are set on offering their carnal critiques of passionate worship. When it happens, don't fret; you are in great company!

A man by the name of David demonstrated passionate worship. Going through a tough spot while trying to bring the glory back to Jerusalem, David hit upon a rather peculiar idea. He would use powerful, abandoned worship to escort God's presence into his life. The story is found in 2 Samuel 6. There are two things I want us to focus on.

First, David possessed absolute abandonment in his worship: "And so it was, when those bearing the ark of the Lord had gone six paces, that he sacrificed oxen and fatted sheep" (v. 13).

It is estimated David and his entourage trekked about five to seven miles while bringing the ark home. That means they stopped about 3,500 times to offer a sacrifice to the Lord. Talk about extravagant worship! David was determined to offer lavish praise to God that day. After all, he wanted MORE of God in his life, so any price was worth it.

I have often wondered about that day. Various scholars attempt to explain away this passionate outpouring, but I really believe David poured it on with all his might. Some may have quit because they thought it was taking too long. Others may have walked away after several steps because they had better things to do. Not David. Let them critique his worship—he was bringing MORE home with him.

Second, we come face-to-face with the most distressing critique, when David came home. Coming into the city, David danced like a wild man. We are told he danced before the Lord with all his might. Exhausted, blood-soaked, his clothes smelling like smoke and gore, David offered God the very best praise he had in him. He danced, whirled, spun, and jumped. In other words, David laid it all out before God.

Watching from a balcony was his wife, Michal. What she saw made her blood run cold. "Then David returned to bless his household. And Michal the daughter of Saul came out to meet David, and said, 'How glorious was the king of Israel today, uncovering himself today in the eyes of the maids of his servants, as one of the base fellows shamelessly uncovers himself!'" (v. 20).

We are told she "despised" what she saw (v. 16). She offered up a critique of disdain, disapproval, scorn. Like so many today who should be caught up in lavish praise for God's goodness every time they have the chance but instead choose to sit back and judge others, Michal rushed headlong to offer her critique of the worshiper. The end result of her bold dash into judgment brought catastrophic results. She, in a very negative curse of her day, was barren the rest of her life (v. 23). She left no mark on history, no lasting posterity.

It is at this point we need to be very careful. If you go back a few pages in Scripture, you will find women coming out to greet David, dancing and singing about his prowess as a warrior (1 Sam. 18:5-7). The church today must fight the tendency we possess to hail a warrior, but harass a worshiper. We are too quick to bless the hard-nosed, driven executive in the Kingdom who "can get things done," while at the same time blasting those who dare to "rejoice like crazy in His presence." I remind you (critiques aside), it was the *worshiping* David, not the *warring* David, who brought MORE of God's presence into Jerusalem. I suspect it will be the worshipers, totally undeterred by the critiques offered by the bystanders, who will be the primary agents of MORE of God's glory being brought to bear in our churches as well. Mark this well—if we set aside (for any reason) our pursuit of passionate worship, we, like Michal, will become nothing more than sterile meeting places where no births into the Kingdom ever occur.

We must be more like David in this aspect: "So David said to Michal, 'It was before the Lord, who chose me instead of your father and all his house, to appoint me ruler over the people of the Lord, over Israel. Therefore I will play music before the Lord. And I will be even more undignified than this, and will be humble in my own sight. But as for the maidservants of whom you have spoken, by them I will be held in honor'" (2 Sam. 6:21-22).

Let's ignore the critics and worship!

Crushed at the Cross

Something else we better prepare for—and this has nothing to do with some carnal church member or caustic pagan hurling insults or spreading rumors—is a renewed vision of Christ that breaks our heart. This one comes straight from the Throne. If we are going to be transformed, changed by MORE from wending sheep into warring steeds, we are going to endure a time of crushing at the foot of the Cross.

Notice a prophetic utterance from Zechariah: "I will pour on the house of David and on the inhabitants of Jerusalem the Spirit of grace and supplication; then they will look on Me whom they pierced. Yes, they will mourn for Him as one mourns for his only son, and grieve for Him as one grieves for a firstborn" (12:10).

This is as pivotal as anything we have thus encountered. In fact, I do not believe a great move of God is coming until we, His people, lie broken before Him in sorrowful repentance. The shallow and trivial ways in which we have come to "enter His presence" have given us a sense of "familiarity" with Jesus to the point He is no longer the Almighty God, Everlasting Father, and Prince of Peace. Instead, He is our best buddy—our pal.

Sorry, but that's not the formula used to describe Jesus, nor the casual demeanor demonstrated when He appeared to those who knew Him best. Consider what happened when the last living apostle, John, witnessed His glory:

> I saw ... One like the Son of Man, clothed with a garment down to the feet and girded about the chest with a golden band. His head and hair were white like wool, as white as snow, and His eyes like a flame of fire; His feet were like fine brass, as if refined in a furnace, and His voice as the sound of many waters; He had in His right hand seven stars, out of His mouth went a sharp two-edged sword, and His countenance was like the sun shining in its strength. And when I saw Him, I fell at His feet as dead. But He laid His right hand on me, saying to me, "Do not be afraid; I am the First and the Last" (Rev. 1:12-17).

John, who incidentally knew what Jesus looked like better than any man alive at that point, fell down like a dead man when the Holy One appeared. So much for frivolous familiarity. I am afraid many of us are in for a shock when we get to the other side! We might do a bit more "carpet time" than we think!

Here's the reality of the situation. God made it clear *He* was going to pour out on His people "the Spirit of grace and supplication" (Zech. 12:10). This will be something of His initiation and it will not be the nice little church service we are accustomed to. As a matter of fact, it will probably scare the daylights out of a large portion of the attendees when it takes place. Here is what God says will proceed MORE . . .

First, *a spirit of grace*. This term really carries the idea of an awareness of God's presence. It is God bending over to grace us with His presence. It is Him making Himself known rather than us depending on the abilities of our performers to entertain us. It is the supernatural being bestowed upon a place where the sick are really healed and the captives are really set free.

Second, the Lord said He would pour out *a spirit of supplication*. Here is where things begin to change in the church. This term usually means the bending of a superior to attend to the need of a lesser. It could be said it is someone with something having pity on someone with nothing. Think of what would happen if in our churches in America we decided we would no longer spend hour upon hour, month upon month, year upon year, clamoring for more stuff in our lives.

Don't get me wrong—I believe in praying for the needs of people. One of the most important parts of a public worship gathering, I believe, is the time when we come together and pray for each other. It is sound, biblical, and it works. But, what do you think would happen if, instead of spending years of meeting "our needs," the church decided to take a month or two and do nothing but pray for, and reach out to, those without salvation? What if, instead of praying for a raise so we can have a newer car or a bigger house, we prayed for a raise so we could give it all to dig wells in Africa or reach lost people in Asia? What would happen to a church that decided it was nice enough, had enough stuff, took good enough care of its members, and instead started focusing on nothing but reaching people who didn't have enough to eat or a place to sleep, or were so marginalized that society at large barely knew they were alive? I can't say for sure, but I have my suspicions He would show up in such a place!

Now for the really tough part: Many comfortable church members in America would already be upset if their church started doing the above. It would be scandalous to many churches to have the influx of people such action would bring. Don't worry, it was scandalous to the church of Jesus' day that He touched such people as well!

It is here, at the next point, where many of us are going to walk away. It is at a fresh revelation of Jesus that a crushing at the Cross takes place. Most of the church world in America today simply isn't ready for such an outbreak of emotion.

Here's what the Lord said would happen: "Then they will look on Me whom they pierced. Yes, they will mourn for Him as one mourns for his only son, and grieve for Him as one grieves for a firstborn" (Zech. 12:10).

This is a powerful image—people wailing as if their only son had been taken from them through death . . . grieving like a firstborn son was snatched away through an accident. In the twenty-five years I have served as a local pastor, I have stood with many families going through the loss of a child. It is a gut-wrenching, emotionally draining experience. I have seen grief put on display unashamed, uninhibited, and unbridled. That is the depth of emotion that will grip us when we catch a fresh revelation of Jesus.

This should create no amazement in us. We have been clearly told that in the final days of earth's history, a vision of the living Christ is going to create pandemonium around the globe: "Behold, He is coming with clouds, and every eye will see Him, even they who pierced Him. And all the tribes of the earth will mourn because of Him. Even so, Amen" (Rev. 1:7).

When that time arrives and He bursts onto the scene to right all wrongs, the vision of Him coming in power and glory will be so unsettling, so disturbing, that men and women around this world will fall into such states of brokenness they will wail, beat their chests, and fall into great mourning. What we don't know about this passage is whether or not they are doing so in repentance or fear over what is about to happen. What we do know for sure is when men and women act so in repentance, grace and mercy flow like rivers. I want to be the recipient of His grace, not His justice!

Exactly how thorough and pervasive will this crushing be? How deep will it run in the church? As we have already seen, it will be thorough. Get ready for some deeply emotional services if the Lord shows up in your church. On top of that, prepare yourself to see people deeply moved whom you have never seen shed a tear. There is a wonderful display of how broad the brush of crushing repentance will be in the next few words from Zechariah:

> "And the land shall mourn, every family by itself: the family of the house of David by itself, and their wives by themselves; the family of the house of Nathan by itself, and their wives by themselves; the family of the house of Levi by itself, and their wives by themselves; the family of Shimei by itself, and their wives by themselves; all the families that remain, every family by itself, and their wives by themselves" (12:12-14).

At first glance, this seems to be a hodgepodge of people repenting. Some names stand out while others are more obscure. However, if you dig a little deeper you will find this represents a broad spectrum of Jewish society. What we are seeing is an entire culture in crushed repentance, from the kingly line of David through the prophetic line of Nathan. Included is the priestly house of Levi and the teaching family of Simeon (Shimei). This strikes a familiar cord with the gifts Paul enumerated—gifts which Christ has given to lead His church. I believe crushing repentance starts with those of us who are responsible for leadership of His body. Naturally, if flows to the remainder of the house. Every family is included. This repentance is far-reaching. However, we as leaders cannot make the mistake of thinking we are somehow aloof, removed from the need to be broken before a new revelation of the Christ. We are to lead the way to Calvary. Following in our tear-soaked footsteps must be the rest of the body of Christ, broken before Him as we have been enraptured by a fresh vision of Christ and Him crucified.

Taking that trek will result in a change in our lives. Even the most astute, powerful among us will be different once we have witnessed Christ afresh. Consider the lifestyle change of a powerful man who was apparently transformed by what he saw on the hill the day they crucified Jesus. "Joseph of Arimathea, a prominent council member, who was himself waiting for the kingdom of God, coming and taking courage, went in to Pilate and asked for the body of Jesus" (Mark 15:43).

Out of nowhere this prominent man was changed. Courage flooded his life. It is no stretch to say Joseph went in and "demanded" the body of Jesus. Here was a prominent member of the Sanhedrin, rich and powerful among the Jews, suddenly demanding from Pilate the body of the Man the same group had seen killed. On top of that, he went in, ignoring all possible consequences, and stood toe-to-toe with the man whose rabid dogs had literally torn the body of Jesus to shreds at various places of torture. All Pilate had to do to exact the very same treatment upon Joseph was to give the order. But this wasn't the same timid, in-the-background, never-take-a-stand Joseph. Something had transformed this meek and mild "Clark Kent" into a "Superman" for Jesus!

The only thing that could have worked this powerful transformation was what Joseph witnessed on the cross that awful day. It was a fresh image of the Crucified One that flipped on the switch and made Joseph of Arimathea the flaming witness he became. The Cross ... the glorious, wondrous, inexhaustible Cross changed him forever.

Recently, I have begun to share with men's groups an apology. My apology basically is that we, the ministry, have tried to draw men into the church with all sorts of nice promises. You know how it runs: Come to Jesus and you will ...

- Have a better marriage
- Drive a nicer car
- Live in a bigger house
- Raise more productive kids
- In other words, live the American Dream.

All that time we have been beating up on men, telling them to be better husbands and better dads, give more to the church, and slice out a little more time for Kingdom activities. We have created ball leagues and tried to entice men with heart-clogging breakfast activities. My first job ever in church was to get up before 6:00 a.m. on a given Sunday, ride my bike to church—I was too young to have a driver's permit—and start calling men to come and eat that Men's Fellowship Sunday.

What I am trying to confess is, I have been there and done that and wondered why my methods were not producing more spiritual men. I now realize the mistake I made and the one we are making in a grand scale. We are trying to allure men (and women) into a spiritual community to take part in spiritual activities without them ever being confronted by the crushing fact we must kneel at the Cross and become one with Him. Somehow we have decided to replace the emotionally exhausting, depths-of-the-soul wrenching experience of falling in complete abandon at that bloody site with a whirlwind of activities and social connections. Regrettably, we are learning that no such replacement efforts will suffice and bring change like clinging to the old wooden beam and the Crucified One.

If our church is going to see MORE come, it will begin with a journey, at least for many of us—not forward into the new vistas of a promising day, but backward, to a place of broken wailing as we realize afresh the reason for His agony and allow the dredging out of our lives, the selfish carnality that has ruled for so long. There is no other way, no other less agonizing path. The question begs to be answered, "Are we willing to take the journey?"

People of Power and Praise

There is one last question we must ask ourselves. It would seem if we have answered the previous questions with an affirming "Yes," this one would be an afterthought. After all, if you have endured the negative catcalls of a postmodern church while daring to say we must go back to a place of His glory and have put up with the eye-rolling and name-calling of those who are critical of your worship, why should any other question bother you? Honestly, if you have groveled at the foot of the Cross to the point you are emptied out and there is nothing left but Him, this should be a piece of cake. However, having endured far too many in-house tussles over demonstrations of power and praise, I know we must hit this final question head-on if we are going to be the recipients of MORE of His glory.

The question is, "Are you willing to become a person of power and praise who brings blessing to others?" Is our church willing to become the place where broken, shattered people come and encounter a living God? Think about your answer before you speak. Remember, when such encounters take place, they are quite often messy, unpredictable, and quite often not all that comforting to the average Joe who is in church today. If you start having this kind of demonstration of His glory, you will probably lose some of the people sitting in your church today. Are you ready for that? Can you trust God to replace them? Are you willing to go through all that will come your way if you start living in this kind of environment? As scary as it seems, the truth is, if we have a true, heaven-sent visitation of MORE of His glory, we have nothing to fear!

Let's look at what God speaks here:

> "In that day I will make the governors of Judah like a firepan in the woodpile, and like a fiery torch in the sheaves; they shall devour all the surrounding peoples on the right hand and on the left, but Jerusalem shall be inhabited again in her own place—Jerusalem. The Lord will save the tents of Judah first, so that the glory of the house of David and the glory of the inhabitants of Jerusalem shall not become greater than that of Judah. In that day the Lord will defend the inhabitants of Jerusalem; the one who is feeble among them in that day shall be like David, and the house of David shall be like God, like the Angel of the Lord before them" (Zech. 12:6-8).

This powerful word concerning the restoration of the Jewish people and Jerusalem carries with it an astounding symbol of what God wants to do with His church. He wants His people to be instruments of power—unstoppable power! Think about the image used here—a firepan in a woodpile and a torch in the dried-out sheaves. As I write these words, the state of New Mexico, indeed the entire Southwest of the USA, is in such a tinderbox state due to drought, it takes virtually nothing to start a wildfire. On a recent preaching appointment, I drove through an area that was so dry it was a fire waiting to happen. On the way back through that area later that same day, someone had grown careless and created a small fire which was being whipped by strong winds. In a matter of just minutes, a wildfire had erupted that was endangering literally miles of dried-up grassland. That—not the mind-set of how we can stop the bleeding of losses around us—is to be the mantra of the church. We are to be consumers, not the consumed. We are to invade our culture, not try to build fortresses that keep the Enemy at bay. Our young men and women are to be salt in a dying carcass, preserving the dignity of God in a perverse world, not squirreled away from the bad stuff out there. We are to be fire, instead of folding up our tents and hoping Jesus comes!

Here's the rub. If you as an individual, or your church as a group, decide to allow MORE to show up so people are touched with the fire, you can expect things to go crazy around your place. It *is* going to get beyond your ability to keep a lid on things. God *is* going to test your limits and boundaries. In fact, He *will* send a few people and circumstances your way to stretch you far beyond the norms of "traditional church." In other words, all those things that mean so much to most of the American church—standing in the community, acceptance among peers, status within the denomination, all those things that are so precious to us today—will be put in a very precarious position.

Before you bolt and say, "I think I will just stay right where I am," consider this. Look closely at what the Lord said. He stated He would save the "tents of Judah [before] the inhabitants of Jerusalem" (v. 7). A tent offers no protection. At least in a walled city like Jerusalem, you were offered some sense of security. Not so in a tent . . .

- Living in a tent means complete vulnerability—no protection from the enemy.
- Living in a tent is reaching the limits of your ability, but pressing on one more step.

- Living in a tent is being confronted by carnal churchmen who threaten your status if you persist in going on in such a passionate pursuit of God, but going on anyway.
- Living in a tent is that group in your church who threatens to leave if you insist on such an "out of control" manifestation of God's Spirit, but remaining steadfast in your insistence.

Is such action dangerous? One might say it is. It has cost many a man of God his position, his livelihood, even his life. But it has also resulted in MORE of God's glory being poured out than the enemy of our soul will ever be able to withstand. Revivals have come because tent dwellers wouldn't quit praying. Healing has come because tent dwellers wouldn't stop anointing with oil and praying prayers of faith. Miracles have come because tent dwellers, who had nothing left to lose, took that one last step of desperation and God thundered from heaven.

So, are you ready to be used in power, to see men and women set free? Are you willing to see alcoholics come stumbling in on Sunday morning as the Lord draws them to deliverance in your altar? Are you willing to give up a Tuesday night sitting at home "vegging out" in front of the TV to go pray for a sick child to be healed, or visit a local jail to see someone delivered from drugs? Is your church ready for a power encounter where the powers of darkness seek to upstage the move of God in your place? What will happen when MORE comes to your church and the feeble, literally those unable to move, suddenly become like David? Think about this one: What will happen when MORE shows up and those who are strong warriors and worshipers like David suddenly become more like an angel of the Most High, imbued with so much of His glory it brings a transformation? If MORE comes, such activities accompany His visit.

Finally, are you ready to become a person, or a place, of praise? We saw earlier that real praise is going to draw the ire of lukewarm church members and the mockery of those who do not know our God. This goes a little deeper. Understand when MORE comes and people start to be set free, there is a natural tendency within us to begin to accept credit for what has taken place. All one needs to do is scan the landscape for all the celebrity pastors and evangelists who live like kings while preaching about the One who gave His all. With their success came men and women who sought to elevate them to a new level. It wasn't long until they actually started believing they deserved such treatment because they were the "man of God." Inflated egos, lavish lifestyles, and a drive to do anything to stay on top have replaced the daily death of the cross.

Pure, passionate praise is the antidote for such excess. Real praise directs all glory back to the One who is deserving. A man cannot bask in the glow of his greatness when he comes before the One responsible for all good things. It is impossible to be arrogant and crushed before the Cross at the same time. Likewise, it is unattainable to allow man's praise to be heaped upon yourself when you are constantly giving praise to the King of kings. A local church cannot be totally focused on itself and be a house of real praise. Those two things are polemic; they cannot exist in the same setting.

That is one of the major reasons we need a fresh release of real praise, not man-made manipulation and craziness of the flesh, but sincere, broken, contrite, honest praise that directs all glory back to God. After all, it really does all belong to Him and we share no platform with Him when it comes to worthiness.

Never forget that, throughout the Word of God, passionate praise always trumps every circumstance. Whether it is Judah being placed at the head of the tribes in the alignment of the nation trekking to the Promised Land, as they were the first to see a new day coming, or David's many failures being overcome because he was a man of praise, true, passionate praise always won out. Whether it might have been Jehoshaphat (sorely outmanned) sending the worshipers out to the battle, or 120 bedraggled followers of Christ worshiping in an upper room when the Holy Ghost was sent swirling into the earth, praisers always came out on top. We still can have MORE if we are willing to deflect praise back to Him and allow Him full access to our lives.

Do we have a long way to go? I can only answer for myself, and the answer is, "Further than I want to admit." However, I know there is a gold mine of glory awaiting us out there if we are willing to make the demanding journey. Let's not settle for church as usual. We have done that too long and are now paying too high a price. Let's band together and witness the transforming powers of God invade our lives and our churches, and stand in amazement at all He does in our midst when MORE breaks forth upon us.

Chapter 8

KEEP COMING!

"So I will strengthen them in the Lord, and they shall walk up and down in His name," says the Lord (Zech. 10:12).

Very few will deny we need MORE of God today. Truthful assessment of the church world reveals painful and telling truths that we are actually at a point of desperation. However, while we know our need, we are reluctant to pursue the path that brings the remedy. Thousands of books are written, millions of dollars are spent going to conferences, and celebrities are created in our midst as we celebrate those who seem to have "figured it out." The whole time the simple truth is right before us; it is just too hard, too time-consuming, too "old-fashioned" for our postmodern world. As threadbare as it sounds, as clichéd as it appears, the rugged old truth is, if we want MORE of God, we have to spend more time coming before Him. That's the great secret of all God's great men and women: time spent before Him. Our question is not one of "if" God is willing or able. We are told with rock-solid confidence we "shall" walk up and down in the name of the Lord.

Victory shall be ours, provided we are willing to keep pressing into the presence of the Lord until He has rained MORE from on high into our lives.

We talk a great deal about prayer—about spending time with God—but we don't really do all that much actual "coming" into His presence. I love the story of three pastors, all meeting on a Monday morning for breakfast, and discussing the sundry ways of prayer. Each had his own specific way of intercession he felt was more effective. While they were having their increasingly heated discussion, for nothing riles us like someone disagreeing with our pet religious beliefs, a telephone repairman sitting in the next booth started eavesdropping.

One minister chimed he was confident that the very best way to have heaven hear your prayer was to fold your hands. He always folded his hands and pointed one finger heavenward as a form of symbolic worship. That, he intoned, was the real way to get through!

Pastor number two, more animated than the first, blared in that number one was all wrong. The real way to effective prayer was kneeling. On one's knees was a sign of real humility, and that's what God requires, was his idea.

Minister number three, feeling pretty good about now, chirped in that the true way to pray was to prostrate one's self before God. Lie out on the floor... stretch out on your face. That displayed real humility and would guarantee your being heard!

Just as they were reaching a discordant crescendo, the telephone repairman, himself a real believer, leaned in and said, "I don't know about you guys, but the most effective posture for real prayer I ever had was dangling upside down by my heels, forty feet off the ground on a power pole!"

I hate to admit it, but I have been guilty of talking a good talk, but not always walking a good walk in this respect. Anyone else feel like repenting with me?

Akin to a Leper

Many of us can identify with a man in the Old Testament. His name was Naaman, and his story is one which relates to the church today on more levels than we would like to admit. Here's what we are told about him: "Now Naaman, commander of the army of the king of Syria, was a great and honorable man in the eyes of his master, because by him the Lord had given victory to Syria. He was also a mighty man of valor, but a leper" (2 Kings 5:1).

Namaan had a great deal going for him. He was riding a high current in life, witnessing some tremendous things, experiencing some glorious blessings. But underneath all the fanfare and glitz, he had this nagging problem: he was a leper.

The Bible gives him some credit where credit is due. Namaan was a physical specimen, for he had strength and prowess . . . but he had leprosy. He was intellectually gifted and knew his way around a battlefield like few men of his day . . . but he had leprosy. There were numerous citations and ribbons attached to the outer shell of his uniform, and he had risen meteorically through the ranks of the Syrian army and had, in all likelihood, a great career ahead of him . . . but he was a leper.

Here's the big deal: Had he been an Israeli, he would have been shelved, ostracized, set apart. But the Syrians didn't care. He had the ability needed for the job at hand, never mind he might be contagious or he might falter because of a sudden onset of weakness. He could get the job done—so cover up the weakness, hide any grotesque appearances, and do what you have to do in order to get the job done!

In reality, Namaan wasn't all that different from many people who will be in church next Sunday. We may not have rotting flesh that is covered over by a nice suit of clothes, but the church is rampant with people who are just covering up debilitating situations every bit as harsh as Namaan's leprosy.

Churches are filled with addicts every week. Drugs, alcohol, pornography, gambling . . . today's list is seemingly endless. We can't let that be seen or someone will have something harsh to say. Couples show up arm in arm on Sunday, but they have fought like tigers through the week and are on the verge of divorce. Of course, nothing can be dealt with because if we come clean and seek God's help in broken prayer, everyone will wonder what's going on and will start rumors. We have an overabundance of families gliding to church in the expensive chariots of our day, dressed in the finest apparel money can buy, but they are headed toward bankruptcy like a skier going down a triple black-diamond slope. No way is help going to be sought here. After all, many of them have been taught to just have the right faith, repeat the right slogans, give to the right people, and God will take care of their compulsive spending addiction without any pain on their part! It would alarm us to be able to look beneath "Namaan's" veneer today and see how many people drearily slide into church on Sunday, depressed and suicidal. Most will never say anything until the communication they left behind is discovered. Then, of course, it is too late.

Like Namaan, I look good on Sunday, until you see the real me. Since I know how you are going to react when you see my "leprosy," I am going to keep it hidden from view with layer after layer of nice-looking religious garments. You are going to think I am the sharpest, most-together, on top-of-life guy you have ever met! But beneath the sham, I am dying!

What makes it worse is the fact I am in the house of healing, but no one seems to be able to reach into my pain and bring me out! It's as if we have decided deliverance is no longer available, so we better develop some real covering and coping mechanisms. Today's church seems to be comprised mostly of preaching (and practicing) cover-up over confrontation; concealment over confession; coping over conquering. Honestly, if all we are going to do is put a nice "religious" spin on the practices of those dead in trespasses and sin, why bother? If all we have to offer is Puritanical hang-ups and some deep-seated guilt, the world doesn't need us. Indeed, as some purport, if that is all we have to offer, they would be better off without us!

There Is Hope!

Fortunately, those stereotypes are not all we have to offer. Those who know our God, the Lord Jesus Christ, can offer more, much more, than those blinded by the god of this world. In fact, we are told something which should raise the bar in all of our lives: "The people who know their God shall be strong, and carry out great exploits" (Dan. 11:32).

If you take the time to really look, the word *exploits* is not in the Hebrew text. It was added to modify the word strong. That word carries the idea of fastening upon something, seizing something, strengthening, curing, and repairing. What the translators were trying to get across to us English-speaking people is this: *When you really know the Lord God, you have the power within you to be strong in the face of the Enemy and bring healing to those around you.*

That's our task today. In the midst of a world that despises us, labels us with epithets, and in the presence of a church that really doesn't want us with them anymore, God has tasked us to be strong, to carry His message of power and deliverance to any and all who will hear!

Enter an unnamed Jewish slave! "And the Syrians had gone out on raids, and had brought back captive a young girl from the land of Israel. She waited on Naaman's wife. Then she said to her mistress, 'If only my master were with the prophet who is in Samaria! For he would heal him of his leprosy.' And Naaman went in and told his master, saying, 'Thus and thus said the girl who is from the land of Israel'" (2 Kings 5:2-4).

I marvel at this young girl. Probably a teen, she had witnessed the shock and awe of invasion. She had suffered the terror of capture and the indignity of deportation. Forced to live in a foreign land, possibly with the image of her parents' death etched forever in her mind, she still held to the Lord God of Israel. I wish I had her tenacity!

She, in the middle of what would cause most of today's American church attendees to curse God to His face, stood her ground and told the story of His power. That power might not be reaching into her life and effecting a miracle for her at that moment, but that didn't mean God wasn't able to do mighty things!

Some of us need to stop and remind ourselves of this little girl from time to time. Just because things aren't going the way we thought they would, the way we hoped they would, does not exclude God from acting in powerful ways around us. You may be trapped in a situation at the moment, and you may have to live in it for a long time, but that does not preclude God from showing His mighty hand right where you are!

She gets word to Naaman, "You don't have to stay the way you are! There is help for you in His presence." There was one condition: he had to get up and go get the blessing of the Lord.

Here's how the story unfolds: "Then Naaman went with his horses and chariot, and he stood at the door of Elisha's house. And Elisha sent a messenger to him, saying, 'Go and wash in the Jordan seven times, and your flesh shall be restored to you, and you shall be clean.' But Naaman became furious, and went away and said, 'Indeed, I said to myself, "He will surely come out to me, and stand and call on the name of the Lord his God, and wave his hand over the place, and heal the leprosy." Are not the Abanah and the Pharpar, the rivers of Damascus, better than all the waters of Israel? Could I not wash in them and be clean?' So he turned and went away in a rage" (vv. 9-12).

His story should clue us in on some requirements to receive God's touch today. The first has to do with *effort*. Naaman had to get up, get permission, gather the caravan, and set out on a journey of some 150-200 miles. Simply put, his provision wasn't going to simply fall into his lap. He was forced to put forth some effort to receive. The second has to do with *expectation*. This great man had his ideas about how church was supposed to be conducted. And, like so many of us, he was rather intransigent in his opinion. It was literally his way or the highway!

It is time for many of us to awaken to the fact the blessing of God we need, the MORE of His Spirit we so desperately lack, isn't going to come via the means we embrace. No man is going to wave his hand over us, speak a "word" to us, or give us a magical formula that will result in God's rich blessing. We have presented for years an image of the superstar minister, jetting into town via his newest custom jet, hidden away in the presidential suite of the most posh hotel, and suddenly entering an arena with the glow of glory emanating from his body. He would bring the answer, provide us with the guidance, and show us the way.

We might as well admit it. We in the Charismatic world of Christianity have been especially gullible in this area. We have packed arenas, purchased millions (if not billions) of dollars' worth of materials, and made servants of Christ appear like rock stars. Leaving these so-called places of worship, we have tried to emulate their methods; we have bought into the slick advertising, and longed for their apparent success.

The problem is, we are discovering all that vivacity we have invested isn't providing what we thought it would. All the words, all the emotions, and all the machinations we have gone through aren't producing a powerful church that is breaking down the gates of hell. It pains me to admit it, but I have gone to some meetings hoping and praying that the man of God could say a word or lay hands on me and I would suddenly discover the might of God for my situation—and left empty!

The problem wasn't the man of God; it was me! I wanted the easy way. I wanted the no-fuss, no-muss method. I wanted the shortcut. And like so many of you, a great number who won't admit it publicly, I discovered the fact that with God, there are no shortcuts. With Him, it really is His way or the highway!

Elisha gave Namaan a simple procedure to follow: "Go dip in the Jordan River seven times and you will be healed." That was it. No great fanfare. No trumpets. No angels singing. Just a simple "get up and go get."

Namaan went ballistic; he threw a fit. His problem was all-too-common. The answer given him was just too simple—too easy, too unreligious. No way could it be of any value. After all, he had better waters to swim in back home than the muddy branch Elisha mentioned. Why in the world would he want to spend time going back to that same old stream that had produced greatness in the past? Like so many, he stormed out, disappointed.

Praise the Lord, that's not where the story ends. In fact, I want to be like Namaan in one more way. While I can readily identify with him on the levels of covering up my problems so no one can see them, and yes, I have left church more than once with a disappointment in my heart, it was his final act that I want so to emulate. Rather than staying mad, the old boy listened and went to the water. After the seventh dip, he was healed. That's the part of the leper from Syria I want to embrace—that seventh dip which brings deliverance.

The All-Important Trip

We are a traveling people. The average American drives twelve thousand miles per year. I guess that means somewhere in America there are eight Americans who don't drive an inch per year because I am logging about one hundred thousand miles myself! Face it, we are busy people.

However, the most important trip I make, or fail to make, is that trip to meet with Jesus. My success or failure depends on that trip. Like Namaan, I can cover up my inadequacies, hoping they don't become too glaring; or, like Namaan, I can finally go to God until His power is revealed in my life. A church can keep on fighting the battle in the flesh, following the dictates of men, or it can sink itself in prayer, going and going until that "seventh dip" is reached and the glory comes. I recently heard it said, "Not one minister who has fallen was ever strong in their daily walk with God, spending time in prayer, at the time of their fall. Not one!" The key to our victory is to follow the imperative the apostle laid before us. "Coming unto Him" must be our most important trip. It is the key to our victory, our very survival.

His Audience Knew the Language

The apostle Peter used language that was familiar to his Jewish audience: "Coming to Him as to a living stone, rejected indeed by men, but chosen by God and precious" (1 Peter 2:4). He used a term that described the priest coming up the steps to approach God, to ascend into the Holy Place to burn incense, to replace the showbread, to oil the lampstand . . . to worship. I see a couple of items that speak to us today.

First, this is *personal*; it is something we have to do for ourselves. It is great to have others pray for us. It is biblical to have others lay hands on us. There is *nothing* wrong with the operation of spiritual gifts, which result in a powerful touch of God being communicated through one to another. However, there are going to be those times when the trip before God must be made by you alone.

It describes a very intimate association between God and the person seeking His face. Through the years, I have insisted on music and some singing during an altar time in church because I want people to be able to express their innermost needs to God without fear of being "overheard" by others intent on making their problems known around town for prayer purposes only, of course!

David shows us how personal, how utterly intimate, this type of coming into His presence must be. In reality, until we can accept this kind of brutal exposure of our lives before God, and maybe even men, the MORE we need will only be a promise, not a reality.

Perhaps you are familiar with David's situation (see 2 Sam. 11—12). It reads like a sordid gossip rag, but it is true. David had fallen prey to his inner demon of lust. Seeing the beautiful Bathsheba exposed and vulnerable, he had to have her. The affair that followed was compounded by an unwanted pregnancy. The cover-up scheme fell through when her husband refused to have sexual relations with his wife while his fellow soldiers lay in the mud of a battlefield. David schemed further and sent orders back with Uriah to have him killed. Imagine that . . . carrying your own death order back to battle! It is hard to believe that David, a man after God's own heart, could sink to such depths, but he did.

Months passed. David sulked. A funeral was held for Uriah. A hasty marriage was sealed. Another funeral was held for a little fellow who had nothing to do with the nasty goings-on. Sorrow pervaded. One day a man of God confronted David—a very brave deed! The resulting words of the musical king have brought comfort to many who have experienced their own fall through the centuries: "Have mercy upon me, O God, according to Your lovingkindness; according to the multitude of Your tender mercies, blot out my transgressions. Wash me thoroughly from my iniquity, and cleanse me from my sin. For I acknowledge my transgressions, and my sin is always before me. Against You, You only, have I sinned, and done this evil in Your sight—that You may be found just when You speak, and blameless when You judge" (Ps. 51:1-4).

Focus in on one line David penned. It was him and God—no one else. Not the woman he seduced, the memory of the man he had killed, not even the heartbreak of a lost son. It was a man and his God.

That's the intimacy that is portrayed before us: a broken, messed-up man or woman who no longer cares for formalities or the words of others . . . church that is tired of chasing the whims and promises of men who don't know a thing about them or their mission, gathering to pour out their hurts and shortcomings before a God who cares and cleanses. Intimacy . . . personal . . . just me and God . . . has to happen before MORE can come.

Second, it's not just a *personal* thing, it's also about *persistency*. Just as the priests never ceased their entrance into His presence, so I must never stop coming into the courts of the Lord. I can remember years back when, in ignorance, we would make a crass remark about someone "riding the altar to heaven." It was a way of throwing a recrimination at someone who dared to come re-enter the presence of God, bringing a persistent need. Back then, in my youthful ignorance (the older I get, the more ignorant I was), we looked down on those who sensed a need to constantly come to God and plead in prayer. In my more recent past, I have stumbled upon a rather humbling discovery: *Every one of us who makes it in will do so because we have grasped an altar and refused to let go!* That's right. Every last person who lives for God for any time at all is going to discover, through education and experience, the absolute need for continual, persistent time in His presence. That's why I urge you: Keep coming into the arena of God's glory. Don't stop. Don't delay. As a matter of fact, put this down and go now!

A Made-up Mind

This issue is settled. I plan to go into His presence over and over. I know I will carry the same needs, say many of the same words, even have those times when it feels as if I am utterly alone and my words simply rattle around the room. As long as I have a need—and from where I stand, that's not going to end any time soon—I am going to get alone, get with some others, find myself a church where I can still spend time with God, and pour out my needs before Him like a priest pouring oil into the lampstand or placing fresh incense into the bowl. I am going to do so because I am convinced I can find somewhere in the depths of Jesus the answer for my sin, my hurt, my hang-up, my weariness, my financial battle. I still believe Jesus hears prayer and has answers!

This appeal to keep coming before Him is based on what I see revealed in the lives of those who dared to come when Jesus strode the dusty alleyways of Israel. Take a moment and notice what happened when some people dared to get up and be personally persistent with Jesus.

- "Behold, a leper came and worshiped Him, saying, 'Lord, if You are willing, You can make me clean.' Then Jesus put out His hand and touched him, saying, 'I am willing; be cleansed.' Immediately his leprosy was cleansed" (Matt. 8:2-3). A leper dares to "come" to Him . . . and leaves totally healed!
- "Now when Jesus had entered Capernaum, a centurion came to Him, pleading with Him, saying, 'Lord, my servant is lying at home paralyzed, dreadfully tormented.' And Jesus said to him, 'I will come and heal him'" (vv. 5-7). A hated Roman centurion dares to break religious and social barriers and "comes" to Him . . . and a servant a great distance away is visited by healing power.
- "Then His disciples came to Him and awoke Him, saying, 'Lord, save us! We are perishing!' But He said to them, 'Why are you fearful, O you of little faith?' Then He arose and rebuked the winds and the sea, and there was a great calm" (vv. 25-26). A band of weary, and less-than-perfect, disciples dares to "come" to Him even though He is sleeping soundly . . . and watch in utter amazement as power that no man has ever displayed issues forth through His words.
- "And suddenly, a woman who had a flow of blood for twelve years came from behind and touched the hem of His garment. For she said to herself, 'If only I may touch His garment, I shall be made well.' But Jesus turned around, and when He saw her He said, 'Be of good cheer, daughter; your faith has made you well.' And the woman was made well from that hour" (9:20-22). A woman whose entire life was damaged goods crashed through the societal and religious barriers and dared to "come" into His dynamic presence,

even to the point of such risk to dare to touch Him ... and left with an answer no man, not even the most educated of the day, could provide.

- "Then great multitudes came to Him, having with them the lame, blind, mute, maimed, and many others; and they laid them down at Jesus' feet, and He healed them" (15:30). Multitudes—literally abundant throngs, even riots—of people took advantage of His presence and "came" to Him, many of them bringing broken, twisted, helpless people, and throwing them at His feet. One after another, they left with amazement as Jesus met them at their point of need and brought healing to them.

Through the New Testament, every time I see people who put forth the effort, who dare to break the barriers, who refuse to listen to the naysayers, and instead "come," they leave with MORE than they came with. That's why I refuse to stop going into His presence. That's why I am going to go back ... and go back again ... and again ... and again—because it is pointed out to me through His Word, if I will keep coming, eventually I will leave with MORE!

Even though I hate to admit this, it is true nonetheless. There are critics who will, as I did in youthful ignorance, point a finger at poor souls such as I, and utter belittling remarks about my inadequacies. I say, "You are probably right!" You can say with integrity, "He's weak." You can put in print with no fear of libel or slander from me, "He doesn't have it all together." Buy an ad in your newspaper and put my photo in there with boxcar headlines, "He's not all he should be!" You won't hear a peep out of me. Call my superiors ... tell them I am not worthy; no news there. I know that better than anyone else on this planet. But here is something you are not going to be able to say with veracity on your part: "He's a mess and too stupid to know what to do about it!" I plan to keep going to the One who has MORE for me until He pours out so much that I, like Jonathan Edwards before me, beg Him to still His hand lest I die.

Chapter 9

A MESSAGE TO THE LEADERS

"My anger is kindled against the shepherds" (Zech. 10:3).

The art of listening is swiftly becoming a lost art. We now live in a "plugged-in" generation where virtually everyone has a set of earphones, or earbuds, in constant use. The result is, we aren't paying much attention anymore. We are distracted, our attention diverted from the vitally important information before us. For instance, if you text while driving, you are six times more likely to be involved in an accident. We simply are not set up to be taking in the information of the road and the cell phone screen at the same time.

Even when it appears we are in position to hear and receive the right information, we can be so distracted there is no way we are actually tuning in. I witnessed this firsthand when going back to seminary to complete the last couple of classes I needed to graduate. I had put off going back for years, actually over a decade. Hence, when I finally made the commitment to go back and complete the course work for a master's degree, I was practically the "father" of the classes. I really had the age difference burned into my mind when I realized I was the only one taking notes the old-fashioned way. I used a pen and notebook, while everyone else plugged away at their computer. Or so I thought!

One day, taking a brief moment to massage the kinks out of my writing hand, I looked up while a professor was making a powerful point. In the midst of his eloquence, I gazed at the computer screen of a fellow student to my left. He was surfing ESPN! I glanced over to some other screens and noted they were plowing through various message boards, game sites, and news feeds. One young lady was working her way through a wedding-planning site. So much for the concern about the "imminent" part of eschatology for her!

Suddenly, it dawned on me. Everyone in the room appeared to be working hard, taking in vital information. All of us were exuding an appearance of eager listening, digesting the vast amount of material being offered. The reality was totally different. We might have given the appearance to an onlooker that we were hard at work. As far as the professor was concerned, we were sponges, soaking up his labor. Even if the president of the seminary had come by and glanced in the window, it would have looked to him like a class full of eager learners who would one day unleash all that powerful theology onto a dying world. The fact was, very few of us were really listening, really hearing what was being said.

The entire message of Zechariah, indeed the pressing need for the Lord to make His appearance and transform His people from wending sheep to warring steeds, came about because the leaders, those entrusted with carrying the power and message of the Almighty, had fallen terribly short in their calling. While God had trusted those raised up to protect the sheep and propel the message (insert the word *church* here for New Testament days), they had fallen asleep at the switch; and although they had the appearance of being rightly positioned and in tune with Him, they were, in fact, at the very heart of the problem. This, according to God,

A Message to the Leaders

wasn't well received in heaven and was going to result in some rather nasty days ahead.

Ring! Ring!

When I was a much-younger man, there was a prophecy preacher who made the rounds in the Church of God. Some who read these words will remember Reverend Albert Batts. Brother Batts would come and spend hours going over detailed explanations of prophecy and their fulfillment. Naturally, those of us who were younger would begin to drift away from his teaching, due to our inability to focus rather than his inability to keep our attention, I assure you! Once Brother Batts noticed us drifting away and doing what all young people did back then—start talking—he would hit a small bell on the pulpit. It would ring out and he would say, "Listen, I want you to get this!" The shrill ringing of that bell would bring us back into focus and we would start listening once again.

We, the church, are hearing a "ring . . . ring" from a bell far more authoritative than that of Brother Batts. I think we are hearing a loud clanging from heaven that the church, entrusted with the message of Christ's cross and coming, is wavering from its real occupation and God has taken notice and isn't pleased. The result is similar to the event described in Numbers 11, where the people tested God by demanding more than His provision. God sent them what they wanted—quail by the ton. But even as they celebrated their success, it turned on them and they were destroyed. The description given by the psalmist is most interesting: "[The people] lusted exceedingly in the wilderness, and tested God in the desert. And He gave them their request, but sent leanness into their soul" (Ps. 106:14-15).

They got what they wanted—quail. But they didn't want what they got—"leanness." This Hebrew term indicated wasting, scantiness. In other words, what they thought they had to have did not produce what they thought it would produce. Rather than growing stronger, bigger, more effective, they declined and grew weaker.

The church, particularly the American church, has invested so much in the last forty years or so, trying to impress the "seeker"—

a better term would probably be the "shopper"—that I fear we have forgotten this whole thing is about the "Savior." God has allowed us to have our way. We have introduced the glitz and glamour of Hollywood, the entertainment value of Broadway, the financial strategies of Wall Street, and the marketing programs of gurus nationwide. He let us do it—and now the church suffers from spiritual anemia and gradual consumption by a pagan culture. I am sure heaven is not that pleased with the way we have allowed the church to fall to such a low estate. I shudder to think about the day when we stand before Him and answer for all our wasted opportunities. Here's the big question: *What are we going to do about it?*

Infestation

> Consecrate a fast, call a sacred assembly; gather the elders and all the inhabitants of the land into the house of the Lord your God, and cry out to the Lord. Alas for the day! For the day of the Lord is at hand; it shall come as destruction from the Almighty (Joel 1:14-15).

Try to find out for certain when Joel wrote his prophetic utterances and you will exhaust yourself. Scholars place him all over the time spectrum of the Old Testament. While the exact date of his message may be hard to nail down, what he teaches is timeless. In essence, Joel told his people there was a great calamity on the way, unlike anything they had ever seen. He compared it to an infestation of locusts, only worse. That was an analogy they understood quite clearly. You and I dismiss such a thing out of hand. After all, what do you do if you find bugs swarming around your house? Buy some bug spray? If that doesn't work, call an exterminator? Failing all else, move!

What do you do when you can't just get up and move? What do you do when the infestation is of "biblical" proportions? That's exactly what Joel had witnessed in his lifetime.

> What the chewing locust left, the swarming locust has eaten; what the swarming locust left, the crawling locust has eaten; and what the crawling locust left, the consuming locust has eaten. . . . For a nation has come up against My land, strong,

and without number; his teeth are the teeth of a lion, and he has the fangs of a fierce lion. He has laid waste My vine, and ruined My fig tree; he has stripped it bare and thrown it away; its branches are made white (vv. 4, 6-7).

Locusts were the bane of an agricultural society. They feared the approach of the locust as much as any American dreads the sirens announcing an F-5 tornado or the constant news reports of a Category 5 hurricane descending upon a coastal city. They harbored such dread with good reason. Locusts are amazing creatures. When food is available, they breed in astronomical numbers. They can lay as many as five thousand eggs in an area of one square yard. There really are no effective means of stopping them once they begin their feeding frenzies.

Called "the teeth of the wind," their invasions leave the landscape bare. Nothing remains. Denuded trees are left to die. Entire regions are stripped bare, devastated. In the early 1950s, a swarm of locusts ate every green thing for literally hundreds of thousands of square miles in Iran, Iraq, Jordan, and Saudi Arabia. Against such power, the people were left helpless.

It was against this harrowing backdrop that Joel rose up and warned of an even greater power coming from the north—a power that was going to rape and pillage the land in a fashion similar to the catastrophe of the locust. Speaking of the invading armies of northern powers—in all likelihood Assyria—Joel called out for the people to prepare themselves for what was on the horizon.

What Does That Have to Do With Me?

For those of us living in the United States, we can easily ask, "What does all this stuff about locusts in the Old Testament have to do with me?" After all, we are living a long way from Joel and his insect-infested contemporaries. We don't fear anyone, or anything. We have this huge economy, even though it has been greatly reduced over the last few years. We have a military capable of dominating any force on the planet. Our technological wizardry is unrivaled. Locusts . . . that's a joke!

Our problem comes when we look at the locust, the existing insect of Joel's day, and think that is the only tool available to God to capture our attention. We contend that there have been several wake-up calls to our nation over the past few years. Sadly, it appears the leadership of our country missed them. Worse yet, it appears the leadership of the church has been equally deaf.

Consider what has happened to our nation over the last decade. We just celebrated the tenth anniversary of the 911 attacks. Who would ever have dreamed a few zealots with box cutters could commandeer a few planes and fly them into buildings? More amazing, who would have ever thought the actions of those misguided individuals would have cost this nation more than $83 billion? Since that hateful day, we have spent more than $100 billion per year on the war on terror. While we are at it, don't let any political party convince you the end is in sight for that outlay. As long as we remain a nation, we are going to make a huge investment in this war. Our country was knocked to her knees when those planes hit and those towers fell. Millions flocked to churches over the next few weeks, and then drifted away. To this day, it haunts me that the American church was so passionless, so powerless, so filled with pabulum in our pulpits; we missed an opportunity to see one of the greatest revivals in history. Sadly, like the man with the tormented son in Mark 9, who brought his pitiful son to the disciples for help but could find none, millions came in the aftermath of 911 to the church bearing the name of Jesus, but they exposed our inability to do anything of consequence. They found us lacking, and walked out en masse.

When Hurricane Katrina hit, we all watched in amazement as the greatest diaspora of Americans since the Civil War, perhaps ever in our history, took place. Like many of you, I raised money, fed hungry people, and did my best to alleviate the suffering. I was moved with pride at the way churches opened their doors and made room for their fellow man. It was wonderful... except for one thing: The spiritual awakening that should have followed on the heels of such an investment of time and material never developed. Here we are, seven years removed from such an opportunity to see revival, and every indicator available tells us we are losing ground.

Those are but two major occasions over the last ten years where the church could have stepped in with Holy Spirit anointing and power and fomented a spiritual revolution. We may have been poised, ready to offer the handout and the lift-up . . . yes . . . but more than that, capable of bringing the Cross and the coming Kingdom into the lives of the broken. Our efforts at disaster relief were heroic, and we should continue to stretch ourselves to the breaking point to relieve suffering. But shouldn't there be more? Should not the church of a living God be able to demonstrate His power, His glory? After all our investments, should there not have been a sweeping of souls into the Kingdom, and tremendous church growth? Have we reached the point in our nation where the church is now only good for disaster relief and compassion on those enduring suffering? Has our message become so lacking, so feckless, we are now good for nothing except for our financial contributions and manpower abilities? In light of the past decade, it seems we have sunk to that very low estate.

A Very Interesting Message

Joel saw what had happened and warned his people a far more disastrous day was coming. It doesn't take a prophet to see dangerous days lie in store for our nation, and our church. In fact, if some of us don't wake up and do what has to be done to bring revival to our land, the American church is going to follow hard on the heels of the European model. Like them, we will become a relic, a testimony to what happens when we have some forms of God around us, but decide we don't want to bother with the power of God any longer.

The Lord spoke through Zechariah to the leaders of his day—the equivalent of our church and her leaders today—and made it clear He wasn't pleased. They had listened to the siren songs of the all-is-well preachers of their day. They had bought into the notion that those on the fringe calling for a wholehearted return to God were lunatics who needed to be ignored or silenced. Because of their willing ignorance of Him, the nation had been turned into a bunch of lost sheep, just wandering along, looking for some direction. God let it be known He was not pleased with their actions and would take matters into His own hands. He would bypass them, make them irrelevant, obsolete. Could it be we in the church are beginning to experience some of that same treatment from God? Could it be our lack of ability to make a difference is because God is setting us aside, making room for another to rise up in our place that will not only do the works of God in compassion, but will also demonstrate the power of God through massive conversions?

It is precisely here that Joel's message becomes very interesting. Flow through the following calls from the throne of God and pay attention to whom the Lord speaks:

- "Hear this, you elders, and give ear, all you inhabitants of the land! Has anything like this happened in your days, or even in the days of your fathers?" (Joel 1:2).
- "Awake, you drunkards, and weep; and wail, all you drinkers of wine, because of the new wine, for it has been cut off from your mouth" (v. 5).
- "Be ashamed, you farmers, wail, you vinedressers, for the wheat and the barley; because the harvest of the field has perished" (v. 11).
- "Gird yourselves and lament, you priests; wail, you who minister before the altar; come, lie all night in sackcloth, you who minister to my God; for the grain offering and the drink offering are withheld from the house of your God" (v. 13).

As I pondered this list of characters, I had to ask myself, *Why this group? What was it about this particular assemblage of people that caused the Lord to have Joel single them out?* You have to admit, it is a rather odd assortment. Suppose today, at a large gathering of religious souls, we paraded before you an elder who was wise beyond compare. After him, we brought up a farmer, strong and determined. Standing beside that duet we assisted a tottering drunk—a sot—and lined him up, as best as he could stand, beside the two distinguished members of our panel. Finally, to add to the luster of the group, we call on a widely read, well-known pastor with a national following. Standing there looking at that scrap iron quartet, you would have to ponder, *What on* earth can there possibly be in that group that would cause God to line them up for our inspection? Knowing our God as we do, we have to come to the conclusion He is trying to get a message across to us. What on earth could He possibly be communicating? Let's take a closer look at each man and see if we can hear something in the background from God.

First, notice the elder. He needs no introduction. He is the wisest, sharpest, most experienced one of the entourage. He has been through the battles, and he knows the ropes. He is experienced and well versed at handling the various situations that arise. He is the type man you want at the helm when a troubling situation arises. He is, sad to say, either in short supply or sadly overlooked in today's church world.

Yet in the calamitous situation before us, even his sage wisdom falls short. Could it be the Lord is trying to tell us our smartest, most seasoned, most politically astute elders are in waters never before experienced? I am convinced the Holy Spirit is trying to communicate to us the message that in spite of our accumulated wisdom from past experiences, human ability simply isn't going to be enough for the future we now face. In other words, we simply don't have the answers within ourselves.

Second, look at the farmer. Farmers are, by nature, a take-the-bull-by-the-horns group of people. They believe in, and daily practice, hard work. They toil, labor, and sweat for every inch of progress. Elders, on the other hand, will sit around a table for days and ponder the various ramifications of a decision.

I think the Lord is trying to tell us that, whereas the elder doesn't have the wisdom to take on the task, the farmer doesn't have the power. We can't "tote that barge and lift that bale" our way out of this one. The days of being busy, frenzied by all the distractions, simply aren't going to produce any longer.

Third (and this one is quite interesting) cast your gaze upon the drunk. This one puzzled me for a long time. I could not, for the life of me, figure out why the Lord would drag such a character before us. What could He possibly be trying to teach us? Then it hit me! A drunk will handle his problems by getting so buzzed, so blasted, he simply forgets about his cares. After all, that's why people drink—for the buzz. God was showing them their ways of handling the issues, particularly the impending disaster on the horizon, wasn't working. They could distract themselves by any means—the drunk used intoxicants—but when the thrill was gone and they came to themselves with a hammering headache, the dark cloud on the horizon was still going to be there.

As much as I hate to admit it, we have all three categories of these people in today's church, and they are here in abundance. We have a great representation of the elder. The American church is rife with leaders who are convinced we can handle our problems with intellectual wit and philosophical strength. If we can just "teach" people to do the right things and "show" people how to overcome the obstacles holding them back, we can build utopia. Mind you, there is nothing wrong with teaching and showing; but we must come back to the fact that people are lost and bound in sin and require more than head knowledge of the Ten Commandments, or so many easy steps to being a better husband. We are confronted with death and destruction that requires an infusion of supernatural power to overcome. Our best and brightest individuals fall short in such a battle.

Of course, we have farmers in abundance. Their mantra is to plan, organize, meet, strategize, implement, follow up, and reshuffle. It is a wearying enterprise! It's almost as if the busier we can get people, the harder we can work at it, and the more sweat produced, the greater we will be.

Don't misunderstand me . . . hard work is vital to a growing church. If you aren't willing to work hard, you won't see any results. That is a biblical principle. However, many of us have tried hard work alone and made a sobering discovery. After we have jumped through all the hoops, done all the required steps, bought the books, listened to the messages, and sent our money, we weren't any better, just tired!

Do you think perhaps it is time for us to step back from our frenzied pace and take stock of what we have done? In spite of our furious level of activity and massive amounts of money and energy invested, we have lost ground in this nation to pagan influences.

We live in a more spiritual age than perhaps any generation in America. Yet there has been so little demonstration of God's power; people by the millions in our land have developed their own syncretic belief system, borrowing a little from Jesus, some from Buddha, a small part of Allah, and covering it over with a hodgepodge mixture of mysticism and humanism. Surely we could see more results from our hard work!

The drunks? They are in fashion today. Sad to admit it, but there are quite a few literal drunks in today's church. But there are far more who want to blunt the harsh news of today's reality by chiming in with a few well-worn clichés. Using excuses such as "The days are evil and many are going to fall away in the last days," we comfort ourselves and make believe there is nothing more we can do. Like the drunken man who doesn't want to face the reality of his life, we choose to ignore the warning signs around us and sit waiting on Jesus to come. It all sounds solidly biblical, until one considers the other side of the last-days equation where God's Word assures us of a last-day outpouring of the Holy Spirit unrivaled in human history. Perhaps we should sober ourselves and seek the new wine!

The Last Man Standing

Now we come to the last man standing, the pastor. I fear it is with us the Lord is most frustrated. We should be leading the charge upon heaven, but based on what the Lord calls on us to do, it is apparent we are missing the mark along the way. I too have been guilty of thinking the elder's wisdom was what I needed most of all. Sitting around the table, hashing things out, strategizing until my furrowed brow ached, I have spent hour upon hour seeking the wisdom of men. There is a part of me who identifies with the farmer as well. Even while sitting in a strategy session, I made notes of all the things I had to get done. And, in a tip of the hat to the drunk, I have more than once used a nice little religious bromide to conceal my apathy and lack of production.

It is to us leaders, people who are in front of God's flock, the Lord calls with a loud and thunderous voice: "Gird yourselves and lament, you priests; wail, you who minister before the altar;

come, lie all night in sackcloth, you who minister to my God; for the grain offering and the drink offering are withheld from the house of your God. Consecrate a fast, call a sacred assembly; gather the elders and all the inhabitants of the land into the house of the Lord your God, and cry out to the Lord" (Joel 1:13-14).

God is simply telling us it is time to once more grow serious about Him. We are in a situation today where our smartest people cannot figure a way out. We are facing a looming threat to the church that our most industrious workers cannot stave off. Our future is too fraught with danger for us to rely any longer on our fanciful dreams and smooth promises. It is time for us to come back to God with our whole heart, to realize our only hope lies in His goodness and grace. It is time for us—the leaders—to abandon the fleshly, carnal, people-appeasing religion that we have adopted and follow the pattern set forth by the Lord.

What God calls for us to do will require surrender. It will require us to abandon our slick status as religious CEOs and adopt the manner of a servant. For so long we have watched with envy as a few have acted like the diviners of Zechariah's day and been the recipients of lavish outpourings from wending sheep. Living in opulence and building vast religious empires upon the backs of the gullible that were desperate for any message of material hope, these so-called prophets have amassed incredible wealth and the accoutrements attached. Jetting in private planes, living in gated mansions, and wearing terribly expensive clothing, they touch the carnal part in each of us and cause—if we are not careful—an envying spirit that will drive us to do whatever it takes to follow in their footsteps. Since they present a slick, nonconfrontational message that attracts crowds and wealth, we feel we must walk in lockstep with them. Nothing controversial will be allowed. Nothing that challenges the carnal mind-set will be tolerated. Everything done must be done with the idea of somehow attracting people to our churches who know nothing of God.

While those principles may work in a church-growth model designed by researchers, it flies in the face of the paradigm of the Owner of the church. Some of you will well remember a couple of decades back when the term "paradigm shift" was in vogue.

A Message to the Leaders

We were hammered constantly with the need to shift, to realign our vision. We did . . . and now we are reaping the benefits of becoming a church that shifted away from a reliance on the power of God and toward the ingenuity of man. Perhaps it is time we "shifted back." That is precisely what Joel called for. Perhaps it is time for us to reassess and realize we are . . .

- Caught in a situation our wisest leaders cannot discern a way out of
- Faced with such a staggering need to reach a lost world that our most industrious workers are falling behind
- Confronted by realities by which our Pollyanna religion, complete with pet phrases and catchwords, is being devoured.

Perhaps it is time we faced reality and admitted what we have been doing simply isn't working anymore—if indeed it ever did—and came back to the methods outlined by the Lord. This won't sell well in the modern school of thought; but could it be the Lord is waiting on us, the leadership, to lay aside our ego and pride and come before Him as Joel called for us to do?

Mark it well—when we do, it won't be pretty. It won't be something we want on television. It won't be something that a select group can control. For sure, it won't have an appeal to those who don't know the Lord nor those who are intent on a nice, comfortable church. But it might ignite a move of God that sweeps thousands into the Kingdom!

What are we called on to do?

- Wail . . . crying out in racking sobs
- Spend the night in an altar . . . not a nice three-minute prayer time
- Fast . . . going without food as a means of humbling one's self before God
- Sackcloth . . . wearing rough garments representing the broken attitude of the repentant
- Solemn assembly . . . not a festive gathering where we celebrate and brag about our accomplishments, but a time of broken repentance

- Crying out . . . loud, boisterous cries where we don't care who is listening or what they think

Try that in most of today's church services, particularly on Sunday morning, and watch as the ushers and leadership run to the closets and bring out the straitjackets and carts for immediate removal from the premises. Or, even more horrifying to those of us in leadership, watch as those who "can't stand such carrying on in church" walk away and seek a more sedate place in which to exert their influence and demand that worship be tailored to their tastes rather than those of a holy, fiery God. Is seeking to find such move of God dangerous? Will trying to have MORE of God and His Spirit present in our services create some issues for us? You had better believe it! The genuine move of the Holy Spirit is a mysterious, often unsettling, and unpredictable thing. It always has been, and always will be. Remember what Jesus said about Him and His work: "The wind blows where it wishes, and you hear the sound of it, but cannot tell where it comes from and where it goes. So is everyone who is born of the Spirit" (John 3:8).

We can no more explain the moving of the Holy Spirit than we can explain the origin, conduct, and departure points of the wind. We can no more control the movements of the Holy Spirit than we can control the raving winds of the tornadoes such as wreaked havoc in the United States in the spring of 2011. And, just as those things caused people to walk away with questions and concerns, so too will a move of God. But this wind will do something the other winds will not. This wind will spread the kingdom of God far and wide and result in conversions that boggle the mind.

Still, we must deal with our fears and our concerns over relevance. But let us not forget the main thrust of this work. Fears and concerns aside, all we are doing now simply isn't getting the job done. It is going to take more, MORE of His glory in our lives, if we are to make a dent in the job before us. A dangerous church, one that assaults and assails the very strongholds of Satan's kingdom, realizes the inability within itself to make any real difference aside from the intervention of the Holy Spirit. Some of us, stepping back and looking at the broader spectrum, have realized we have about the same chance of seeing thousands, hundreds of thousands, of people set free without the dynamic move of the Holy Spirit as the farmers of Joel's day did of killing a billion locusts with a hoe. We have reevaluated and determined that without heartfelt repentance and brokenness before God, we have about the same chance of getting God's attention as they did of stopping a locust plague by plowing a little deeper furrow with their farming instruments. Our attempts to defeat the Enemy, Satan, now seeping deeper and deeper into our culture, will be repelled by our human machinations like they repelled the marauding Assyrians by standing at the border and throwing rocks. It is going to take MORE. Not just more work, more training, more relevance, whatever that means. It is going to take more of *Him*!

Here's the glorious promise: If we will position ourselves before Him, cry out with our whole heart, and be broken in His presence, He has already assured us, MORE is available, and MORE will come! We don't have to continue to slug things out in the flesh. We can witness an outpouring of His glory that rivals anything we have ever seen or ever heard of. Do you doubt that statement? Do you believe things are too far gone? Remember the staggering statement made by the apostle Paul: "Now to Him who is able to do exceedingly abundantly above all that we ask or think, according to the power that works in us, to Him be glory in the church by Christ Jesus to all generations, forever and ever. Amen" (Eph. 3:20-21).

If you can dream it, He can do it with ease! If we can pray it, He can perform it! And, when it becomes more about His glory than our advancement, He will!

Don't give up. Don't shrug off your family as hopeless. Don't write off your church as too far gone. And whatever you do, don't turn your back on this country, simply handing it over to the pernicious forces of darkness which today seem to run unabated. Our God is still in heaven and will still answer the broken sobs of His people. He can yet show up in our churches and pour out MORE. He can once more rock this nation with revival, just as He has done in days gone by.

In the late 1780s, revival broke out along the American frontier—at that time, Kentucky. Men like Francis Asbury and Peter Cartwright, borne on horseback, had pressed into the wilderness, carrying the passion and flame of Jesus Christ with them. Around 1800, a Presbyterian minister by the name of James McGreedy rode into south central Kentucky for a four-day meeting. From about a one hundred-mile radius, people showed up, bringing their tents, and the camp meeting concept was born. What's more, the Holy Spirit showed up with MORE.

There, with a motley mixture of different ministers, the Lord poured out His glory. According to those in attendance, things happened that baffled description. Many fell down like they had been killed in a battle. Moans and shrieks would fill the air as grown men and women cried out for mercy from heaven. Sober church members—those who, like us, had seen it all—began to be broken. They would testify how in days past they would have despised anyone who acted as they were now acting. No longer was that their mind-set. They had encountered MORE on the prairie. In fact, a Methodist minister, John McGee, when surrounded by preaching that was filled with such power and boldness, overcame his reservations and moved with urgency and ecstasy, preaching the powerful Word of God until the place was littered with men appearing slain before our Holy God.

Revival came to America then. And revival can come to America again. God is looking for some leaders unafraid of the snickering mockery of the religious establishment who wish only to see their fame grow. He is searching for some leaders who are unafraid of the stony, flint-like faces of men and women occupying pews who want nothing to do with a fresh outpouring of His glory. He is looking—thoroughly searching us out—for some men and women who are willing to be broken between the porch and the altar, and then rise up and lead people into MORE of God's glory and power. The question is not, Can it happen? The question is, Is this going to happen to us?

My prayer is that we become conduits through which His glory can flow; that you become so anointed, your life breaks forth into another dimension; that our churches become houses of prayer once more and that we would see another wave of God's power sweep from coast to coast; that you and I encounter MORE!